Interest-Rate Options

INTEREST-RATE OPTIONS

Brian Coyle

FINANCIAL WORLD Publishing

THE CHARTERED INSTITUTE OF BANKERS

Financial World Publishing
IFS House
4-9 Burgate Lane
Canterbury
Kent
CT1 2XJ
United Kingdom

Telephone: 01227 818687

Financial World Publishing publications are published by The Chartered Institute of Bankers, a non-profit making registered educational charity.

Typeset by Kevin O'Connor
Printed in Italy

ISBN 0-85297-442-6

Contents

Financial Options

An Option Agreement

An option is an agreement between a buyer (the option holder) and a seller (the option writer) that gives the option holder:

- the right, but not the obligation,
- either on a specified date, or on or before a specified date (the expiry date or exercise date)
- to buy (call option) or to sell (put option)
- an underlying item
- at a fixed price (the exercise price, strike price or strike rate).

The option holder acquires this right by purchasing the option. The purchase price is known as the premium.

For example, an exploration company could have an option to drill for minerals on a piece of land or employees could hold options to buy shares in their company at a specified price. Financial options, such as interest-rate options and currency options, give the option holder the right to buy or sell a specified financial instrument.

If the option holder exercises his/her right, the option writer is obliged to carry out the terms of the agreement, and must either deliver the underlying item to the option holder at the agreed price, or pay an amount of cash to the option holder in compensation.

If the option holder chooses not to exercise his/her right, because a better price is available for the underlying item in the cash market, nothing needs to be done, and the option will lapse at its expiry date.

A call option secures a worst-possible buying price and a put option secures a worst-possible selling price for the underlying item. The buyer of an option, by guaranteeing a worst-possible price, is obtaining some certainty about the future price of the item. The option writer is taking on price risk from the option buyer in exchange for the premium.

Options are more likely to be wanted when there is uncertainty about the future market price of the underlying item because this price is volatile.

The Underlying Item

An option is a derivative instrument because it is an agreement whose value is related to or derived from another, underlying item. The underlying item can be anything with a market value. In the case of financial options, the underlying item is a financial product or instrument. This might be:

- a quantity of shares (equity option)
- a notional portfolio of shares (a stock index option)
- a quantity of one currency that is exchangeable into another currency (a currency option)
- a notional loan or deposit (an interest-rate option)
- a futures contract (an option on a future).

OTC Options and Exchange-Traded Options

Options can be either over-the-counter products or exchange-traded.

- An over-the-counter (OTC) option is negotiated directly between the buyer and the option writer that is usually a bank. The terms of the agreement can be tailored to the specific requirements of the option buyer.

- An exchange-traded option is a standardized agreement whose terms are specified by the exchange on which it is traded. Options are available at a number of exercise prices.

Traded options include equity options and options on futures. Interest-rate options are OTC options, with the exception of options on interest-rate futures.

Call Options and Put Options

Options are either calls or puts.

A **call option** gives its holder the right to buy the underlying item at the exercise price, and obliges the option writer to sell the item at that price if the option is exercised, or to make a cash payment to the option holder in compensation.

A **put option** gives its holder the right to sell the underlying item at the exercise price, and obliges the option writer to buy the item at that price if the option is exercised, or to make a cash payment to the option holder in compensation.

The underlying item might be a notional item, such as a notional loan or a notional portfolio of shares. An *interest-rate call option* gives its holder the right to obtain a notional (interest-paying) loan at a fixed, predetermined rate of interest. An *interest-rate put option* gives its holder the right to obtain a notional interest-earning deposit at a fixed, predetermined rate of interest.

In the event of an interest-rate option being exercised, the option writer settles his/her obligations by making a cash payment to the option holder, rather than by delivering the item to the option holder at the agreed price.

A call option might be purchased by an organization wishing to secure a maximum future purchase cost for the underlying item. The actual purchase cost that an option secures is the lower of:

- the strike price (exercise price), in the event that the call option is exercised, and
- the actual market price for the item, when this is lower than the strike price and the option is allowed to lapse.

Similarly, a put option might be purchased by an organization wishing to secure a minimum future sale value for an underlying item. The actual sale price that an option secures is the higher of:

- the strike price (exercise price), in the event that the put option is exercised, and
- the actual market price for the item, when this is higher than the strike price and the option is allowed to lapse.

An interest-rate option sometimes is called an **interest-rate guarantee**, because it guarantees a worst-possible interest rate for the option holder.

A call option also might be purchased by an individual or organization speculating on a rise in the market price of the underlying item, so that by the expiry date for the option, the market price is higher than the option's strike price. The option then can be exercised to earn a profit for its holder. Similarly, a put option might be purchased by someone speculating on a fall in the market price of the underlying item.

American-Style and European-Style Options

An option has an expiry date or expiration date as it is sometimes known. If it is not exercised by a stated time on its expiry date, it lapses, and the rights of the option holder and the conditional obligations of the option writer cease.

- An **American-style** option may be exercised at any time up to and including its expiry date.
- A **European-style** option may be exercised on its expiry date only, and not before then.

The terms American and European have no geographical significance.

Both types of option are readily available around the world.

Strike Price (Exercise Price)

The strike price, or exercise price or strike rate, for an option is the price at which the option holder can buy (call option) or sell (put option) the underlying item.

For OTC options, the strike price is negotiated between the option buyer and the option writer. An option writer (a bank) will agree to whatever strike price the option buyer wants, provided the option buyer is willing to pay the premium quoted.

Exchange-traded options are available at a number of different strike prices, above and/or below the current market price of the underlying item.

The strike price is expressed in the same way as the price of the item.

- For an equity option, the strike price is a share price.
- For a stock index option, the strike price is a stock index level (number). The strike price is negotiated between the option buyer and the option writer: an option writer (a bank) will agree to whatever strike price the option buyer wants, provided the option buyer is willing to pay the premium quoted.
- For a currency option, the strike price is an exchange rate.
- For an interest-rate option, the strike rate is a benchmark interest rate, such as the three-month sterling LIBOR rate or the three-month European Bankers Federation euribor rate.
- An option on a future is priced in the same way as the underlying future.

Example

An organization buys a call option on a (notional) three-month loan of $10 million. The strike rate is 6.75%, and relates to the three-month eurodollar interest rate.

Analysis

The option holder has obtained the right to pay interest at 6.75% on a three-month loan, starting on or before the expiry date for the option. This fixes a maximum borrowing cost. If the three-month eurodollar rate is above 6.75% on expiry, the option will be exercised, and the interest rate of 6.75% will be obtained. If the eurodollar rate is below 6.75% on expiry, the option holder will let the option lapse, and will borrow at the lower available market rate.

In-the-Money, Out-of-the-Money and At-the-Money Options

When an option is written, the strike price might be above or below the current market price for the underlying item. The relationship between the strike price and the market price will be a factor that contributes to the size of the option premium.

- When the strike price for an option is more favorable for the option holder than the market price for the underlying item, the option is **in-the-money**.
- When the strike price for an option is less favorable to the option holder than the market price for the underlying item, the option is **out-of-the-money**.
- When the strike price is exactly the same as the price of the underlying item, the option is **at-the-money**.

The extent to which an option is in-the-money or out-of-the-money varies between the time the option is first written and its exercise date. This is because the price of the underlying item is changeable, and will move up and/or down. An option might change from being out-of-the-money to in-the-money, or could move from in-the-money to out-of-the-money.

In-the-money options	Out-of-the-money options
An option that is in-the-money when it is first written will be more expensive to buy than an out-of-the-money option identical in all respects except for its strike price.	Out-of-the-money options are cheaper than comparable in-the-money options.
An option will be exercised only if it is in-the-money.	If an option is out-of-the-money at expiry, it will not be exercised, and will be allowed to lapse.
An option that is deeply in-the-money will be more valuable for its holder than an in-the-money option whose strike price is just about more favorable than the market price of the underlying item.	An option that is deeply out-of-the-money will be worth much less to its holder than an out-of-the-money option whose strike price is slightly less favorable than the market price of the underlying item.
An option that is deeply in-the-money is likely to be exercised at or before expiry.	An option that is deeply out-of-the-money is unlikely to be exercised at expiry because a very large change in the market price of the underlying item is required before it will become in-the-money.

Options can range from deeply in-the-money to deeply out-of-the-money.

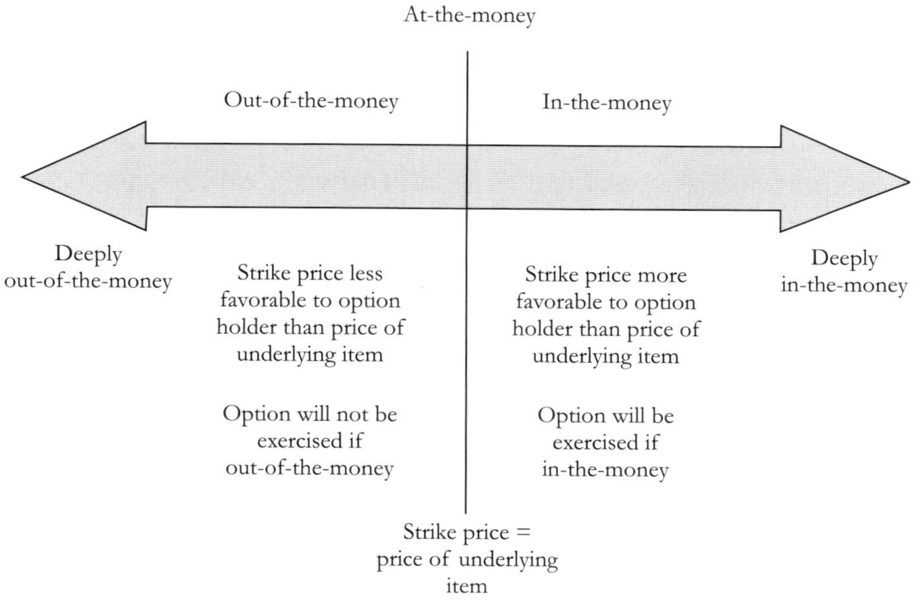

Example

A European interest-rate call option is written, giving its holder the right to borrow a quantity of funds at 4% for three months. A European interest-rate put option is written, giving its holder the right to deposit a quantity of funds at 4% for three months.

The benchmark rate of interest for both these options is the EBF three-month euribor rate.

Strike rate	Euribor rate at expiry	Call option	Put option
4%	Above 4%	In-the-money	Out-of-the-money
4%	4%	At-the-money	At-the-money
4%	Below 4%	Out-of-the-money	In-the-money

The benchmark rate of interest (the market price of the underlying item) should be seen as the interest rate at which the call-option holder can borrow funds and the put-option holder can deposit funds.

In this example, when the euribor rate is over 4%, the call option is in-the-money because the cost of borrowing is above 4% but by exercising the option, the option holder secures a borrowing cost of just 4%. On the other hand, when the euribor rate is above 4%, the put option is out-of-the-money because the option holder can obtain a better rate of interest by depositing funds at the euribor rate than at the strike rate of just 4%.

In this example

- the call option will be exercised at expiry if the euribor rate is above 4%
- the put option will be exercised at expiry if the euribor rate is below 4%.

This example also might help to illustrate that when a call option is in-the-money, a put option on the same underlying item and at the same strike price is out-of-the-money by the same amount. Similarly, when a call option is out-of-the-money, a put option on the same underlying item and at the same strike price is in-the-money by the same amount.

European Interest Rate Options: the Meaning of 'In-the-Money'

For interest-rate options, the underlying item is a notional loan (call option) or deposit (put option) and the strike rate is a benchmark rate of interest. However, the rule for deciding whether an American-style option is in-the-money or out-of-the-money differs from the rule for European-style options. An **American** option can be exercised at any time to expiry, so it will be in-the-money if its strike rate is more favorable than the current spot market rate of interest.

A **European-style** option can be exercised only at the expiry date. It is therefore in-the-money if the strike rate is more favorable to the option holder than the interest rate that could be obtained now for a loan or deposit starting at a specific date in the future (the exercise date). This is the interest rate available on an appropriate forward-rate agreement or

FRA. A European interest-rate option therefore might be described as an option on an FRA.

An FRA is an agreement in which the buyer undertakes to acquire a notional short-term deposit from a future date (settlement date) at a fixed rate of interest. The seller of the FRA undertakes to provide the notional deposit, i.e. pay for funds, at this fixed rate.

- The strike price for an interest-rate call option therefore is comparable with the price obtainable for selling an FRA for the same notional interest period.
- The strike price on an interest-rate put option is comparable with the price obtainable for buying an FRA for the same notional interest period.

Example
Now is February 1. An organization buys a European-style call option on a notional three-month loan of $10million, at a strike rate of 6%, with an expiry date of 1 April.

On 1 February, an FRA could be arranged on a notional three-month deposit of $10 million, at an agreed (fixed) rate of interest, for settlement on 1 April. Settlement date is the first day of the three-month notional deposit period.

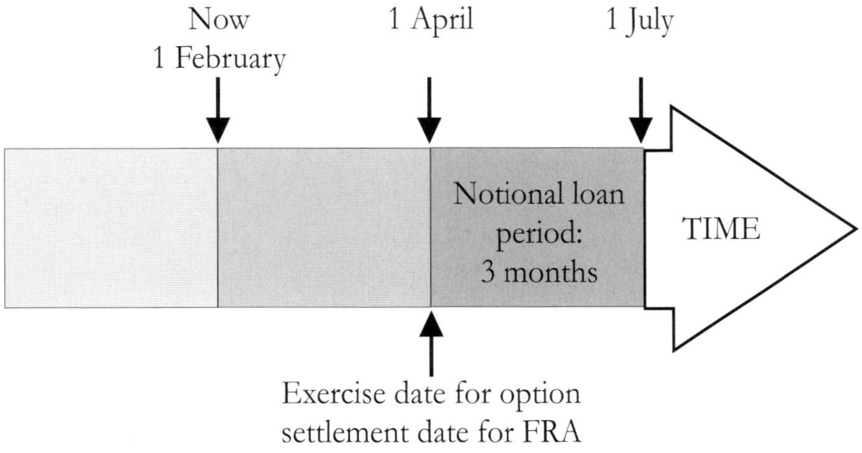

The FRA is a 2 v 5 FRA as at 1 February because the notional deposit period starts in two months and ends after five months. The European option can be described as an option on the FRA.

- If the FRA rate is below 6%, the option is out-of-the-money when it is written on 1 February, because a better borrowing rate can be obtained at this time by selling an FRA.
- If the FRA rate is above 6%, the option is in-the-money when it is written because a better borrowing rate will be obtained by exercising the option at expiry than by selling an FRA on 1 February.

Interest-rate option (European)	Option strike rate higher than FRA rate	Option strike rate lower than FRA rate
Call option	Out-of-the-money	In-the-money
Put option	In-the-money	Out-of-the-money

Premium

The premium for an option is its purchase price. Option prices are considered in more detail in a later chapter, but some aspects of price are introduced here.

The price of an option has to be acceptable to both the buyer and the writer. If the premium favors either the buyer or the writer, there would be no option transactions. Option-pricing models are used to calculate option prices. A number of option-pricing models are in use: all are based on similar assumptions.

Logically, it might be apparent that the size of an option premium will depend, to a large extent, on three factors:

- the relationship between the strike price and the market price of the underlying item, the extent to which the option is in-the-money or out-of-the-money when written
- the time to expiry of the option
- the price volatility of the underlying item.

The current value of an option will vary over time, from when it is written up to its expiry date. Its current value at any time will depend largely on these same three factors.

Relationship between Strike Price and Market Price of the Underlying Item

The premium for an option will depend on whether the option is in-the-money or out-of-the-money, and by how much. In-the-money options will cost more than out-of-the-money options, because they have a greater chance of being in-the-money, and more deeply in-the-money, at expiry.

- A call option to borrow funds at 5% will cost more than a similar call option to borrow funds but at a strike rate of 6%.
- Similarly, an interest-rate put option giving its holder the right to deposit funds at 5% will cost more than a similar put option to deposit funds, but at a strike rate of just 4.5%.

The relationship between an option premium and the extent to which the option is in-the-money or out-of-the-money is perhaps most easily illustrated with an example of traded equity options. A traded equity option gives its holder the right to buy (call option) or sell (put option) a quantity of shares in a company at a fixed price, the exercise price. Traded options might be available in shares of ABC Corporation as follows:

Company: ABC Corporation
Current share price: 244

	Calls		**Puts**	
Exercise date	**July**	**October**	**July**	**October**
Exercise price				
220	44.5	47.5	8.5	21.0
240	26.5	39.5	20.5	30.5
260	17.0	30.5	31.5	41.5
280	2.5	20.0	51.0	60.5

Time to Expiry and the Option Premium

The premium for an option with a longer remaining term to expiry always will be higher than for an option identical in every respect except with a shorter remaining term to expiry.

This is because there is a longer remaining time in which the market price of the underlying item can move, or move further, in the option holder's favor.

This is the case for both American and European options, although the logic of this time value of options is probably more apparent for American-style options than for European options.

Suppose, for example, that two American options are written on the same date and are identical in every respect, except that Option A expires two months before Option B. Option B offers all the benefits of Option A, and can be exercised if required on any of the dates that Option A can be exercised. In addition, Option B can be held for two months longer, and exercised at a later date if required. The buyer of Option B therefore should pay more than the buyer of Option A.

Volatility in the Price of the Underlying Item

The premium for an option will be higher when the price of the underlying option is more volatile. Price volatility creates uncertainty about future price movements and price risk. Options are financial instruments for trading price risk: the option holder pays to offload price risk to the option writer. A higher premium is required to persuade an option writer to take on the price risk.

Premiums for European and American Options

It might seem logical to suppose that the premium for an American option should be higher than the premium for a comparable European option because an American option offers greater flexibility of exercise dates.

In practise, this is not the case because the value of an option depends not just on the difference between the strike price and the current market price of the underlying item, but also on the remaining time to expiry. If an American option is exercised before its expiry date, it loses all its time value. American options therefore usually are allowed to run to expiry, and so are used in much the same way as European options.

The premium for an American option consequently will be similar to the premium for a comparable European option.

Exercising an Option

An option holder has the right but not the obligation to exercise the option. The choice of whether or not to exercise the option rests entirely with the option holder, and the decision to exercise it will be taken if the option is in-the-money at expiry.

The holder gives notice of an intention to exercise the option by the latest time specified in the option agreement. The latest time for notification is usually one or two business days before settlement date.

Settlement

When an option is exercised, the option writer must carry out the obligations under the terms of the option on settlement date. The nature of settlement differs according to the nature of the option.

- Some options are settled by *physical delivery* of the underlying item by the option writer to the option holder, and payment for the item from the option holder to the writer.
- Other options are settled by means of a *cash payment* from the option writer to the option holder. The size of the payment depends on the nature of the underlying item, and the difference between the strike price and the market price of the

underlying item at its exercise date. The cash settlement of option agreements is knows as settlement for difference. Interest-rate options, with the exception of options on interest rate futures, are settled in this way.

Types of Interest-Rate Option

There are various types of interest-rate option. The following chapters describe

- borrowers' and lenders' options that are OTC options
- interest-rate caps, floors and collars, and captions that are also OTC options
- options on interest-rate futures that are exchange-traded on the same exchange as the underlying futures contracts.

Interest-Rate Option

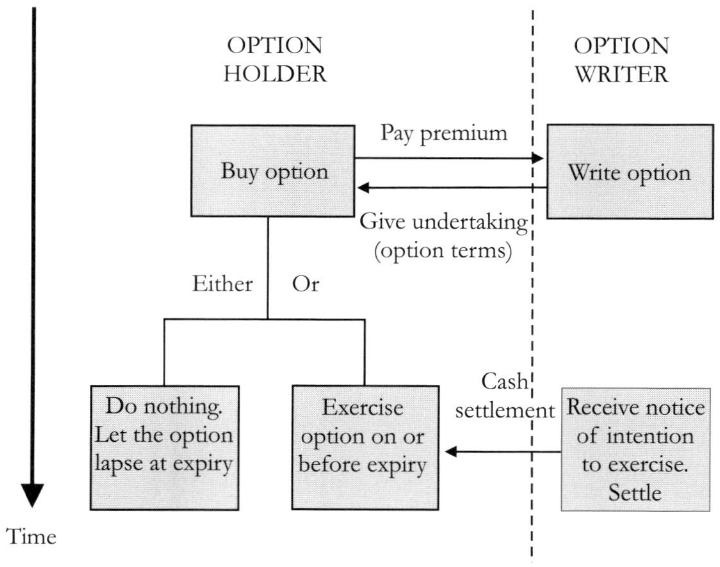

Borrowers' and Lenders' Options

Borrowers' and lenders' options are interest-rate options (interest rate guarantees) on a short-term loan or deposit. They are OTC instruments, and are negotiated between the buyer and an option writer (bank).

- A borrower's option is a call option on a notional short-term loan with a starting date at some time in the future. Buying a borrower's option guarantees a maximum borrowing cost for the option holder.
- A lender's option is a put option on a notional short-term loan with a starting date at some time in the future. Buying a lender's option guarantees a minimum lending rate or investment yield for the option holder.

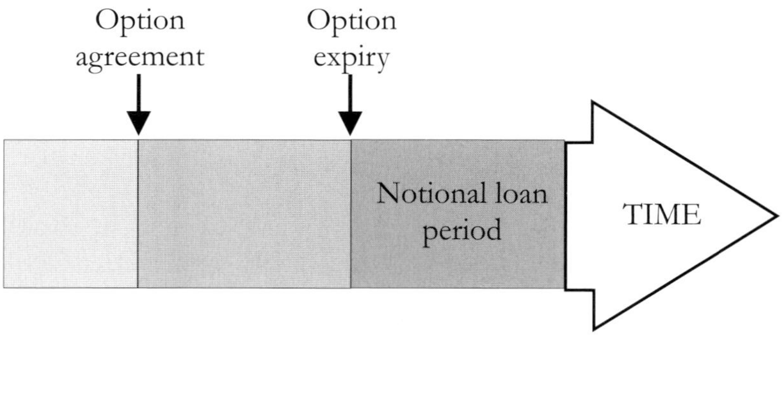

For both borrowers' and lenders' options, the underlying item is a **notional** loan starting at a specified future date. This notional loan

- is for a specified principal amount

- for a specified term/maturity
- with interest payable at a recognized benchmark rate, specified in the option agreement such as two-month EBF euribor rate or the three-month dollar LIBOR rate, etc.

The rate of interest payable, as a percentage amount, is the option strike rate.

Options on an FRA

The underlying item for a borrower's option and a lender's option is, in effect, a forward-rate agreement or FRA. An FRA is a binding contract between a buyer and seller for which the underlying item is a notional deposit on a specified principal amount, starting at a future date and for a set term, on which the interest is receivable at a rate fixed in the FRA agreement.

Borrowers' and lenders' options are options on notional loans. FRAs are contracts on notional deposits.

- An organization wishing to fix a future rate of interest for a short-term loan could sell an FRA. Alternatively, it could obtain an option on fixing a future rate of interest on a loan by purchasing a borrower's option.
- An organization wishing to fix a future rate of interest income on short-term lending or a short-term investment could buy an FRA. Alternatively, it could obtain an option on fixing the future income yield by purchasing a lender's option.

A borrower's option therefore can be described as an option on selling an FRA, and a lender's option can be described as an option on buying an FRA.

Lenders' and Borrowers' Options as Interest-Rate Guarantees

Borrowers' and lenders' options are options on a notional loan, not options on an actual loan. There is no intention or arrangement between the option buyer and the option writer that a loan or deposit will be arranged if the option is exercised.

It is more appropriate to regard borrowers' and lenders' options as options on an interest rate. A borrower's option is an option to borrow at a fixed rate of interest, and therefore it guarantees a maximum interest cost. A lender's option is an option to lend or invest at a fixed rate of interest, and therefore it guarantees a minimum interest yield.

Borrowers' Options

A borrower's option gives its holder the right, but not the obligation, to obtain a notional loan on a specified principal amount at a fixed rate of interest that is the strike rate for the option. The notional loan has a specified starting date (at expiry of the option) and a fixed maturity.

The terms of the option agreement provide for a cash settlement, settlement for difference, in the event that the option is exercised.

When a borrower's option is exercised, the amount of the cash settlement represents the difference in cost between borrowing the principal amount for the loan term at the strike rate, and borrowing the money at the current benchmark rate of interest at the option's expiry.

To compare the strike rate with the benchmark rate of interest, the benchmark rate of interest must be strictly defined, i.e.

- which benchmark rate of interest should be used, and
- how should an actual rate of interest be attributed to this benchmark rate when the option reaches its expiry.

Example
A European-style borrower's option is arranged on a notional three-month loan of £8 million, starting on 1 October. The benchmark rate of interest is the British Bankers' Association three-month sterling London Interbank Offered Rate. The strike rate for the option is 5.75%.

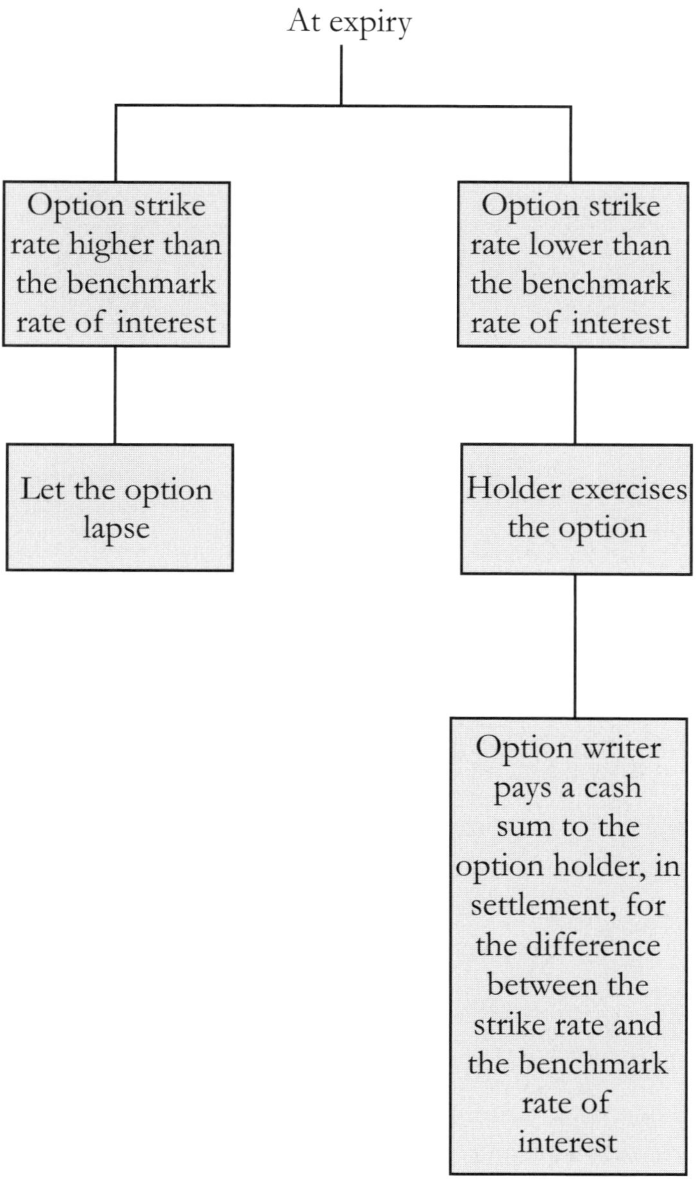

The option agreement states that if the option is exercised, the strike rate will be compared with the three-month LIBOR rate as at 11.00 a.m. two business days before 1 October, and settlement will take place on 1 October.

Analysis
Two business days before 1 October, the option holder will compare the current BBA three-month LIBOR rate with the option strike rate. If the LIBOR rate is higher than the strike rate of 5.75%, the option holder might be required to notify the option writer of an intention to exercise the option. Alternatively, the option agreement might provide for the option to be exercised automatically without the need for formal notification by the option holder to the option writer. However, it is normal for formal notification to be given by the option holder.

On settlement date, the option writer will make a cash payment to the option holder for the difference in the interest cost on a loan of £8 million at the strike rate of 5.75% and on a loan of £8 million at the three-month LIBOR rate.

Fixing a Maximum Borrowing Cost

A borrower's option can be used by an organization that is intending to obtain a short-term loan at some time in the future. The option can be used to hedge the organization's exposure to interest-rate risk, i.e. to the risk of an unexpected rise in the general level of interest rates.

Example
A European organization expects to raise a six-month loan of $25 million on 1 November. It can borrow at the six-month dollar LIBOR rate plus 1%. The six-month dollar LIBOR rate is currently 5%, but the organization is concerned that the rate could rise to 6% or even higher before 1 November.

It would like to arrange a hedge against the risk of the borrowing cost rising above a certain level, but does not want to lock in a fixed borrowing cost by selling an FRA.

Suppose the organization wants to fix a maximum effective borrowing rate of 6.25% for the loan by purchasing a borrower's option. Because the organization will borrow at LIBOR plus 1%, a strike rate of 5.25% for the option will guarantee a maximum borrowing cost of 6.25%.

(Note: This example ignores the cost of the option premium. It is assumed that the organization wishes to guarantee a maximum borrowing cost of 6.25% exclusive of the option premium cost.)

The organization discusses its requirements with a bank that is a writer of interest-rate options. It buys a borrower's option on a notional six-month loan of $25 million, with an expiry date of 1 November. The benchmark rate of interest is the bank's six-month dollar LIBOR rate and the strike rate for the option is set at 5.25%.

Analysis
At the option's expiry, the six-month dollar LIBOR rate might be higher or lower than the option strike rate of 5.25%.

Outcome 1: benchmark rate higher than strike rate
Suppose that the six-month LIBOR rate at expiry is higher at 6.0%.

- The organization will borrow $25 million at dollar LIBOR plus 1%, i.e. at 7.0% for six months.
- The option will be exercised, and at settlement the option writer will pay the organization a cash sum for the 0.75% difference between the cost of borrowing at the six-month LIBOR rate (6.0%) and the cost of borrowing at the option strike rate (5.25%).

	%
Borrow at	7.00
Compensation on settlement of option	-0.75
Net effective borrowing cost	6.25

The effective borrowing cost, 6.25%, is the maximum borrowing cost that was guaranteed by the borrower's option.

Outcome 2: benchmark rate lower than strike rate
Suppose that the six-month LIBOR rate at expiry is lower at 4.75 %.

- The organization will borrow $25 million at dollar LIBOR plus 1%, i.e. at 5.75%, for six months.
- The option will not be exercised.

The borrowing cost is lower than the maximum rate guaranteed by the borrower's option. This is because the option has not been exercised, and the option holder has taken advantage of the more favorable level of market interest rates at the option's expiry date.

This example should illustrate an important feature of a borrower's option.

- A borrower's option guarantees a maximum borrowing cost.
- Ignoring the cost of the option premium, a lower borrowing cost will be achieved when the option is not exercised because the benchmark interest rate is below the strike rate at expiry.

A borrower's option therefore sets a limit on the downside risk by guaranteeing a maximum interest cost but allows the option holder to benefit from a favorable market-interest rate at the option's expiry date.

The Option Premium and the Effective Borrowing Cost

The net effective borrowing cost for the buyer of a borrower's option should take into account the cost of the option premium. This is paid by the option buyer up front when the option is written, regardless of whether the option subsequently is exercised or not. It is a cash sum, but the cost of the option can be converted into an equivalent borrowing cost, applied to the notional loan.

Cost of option, as an equivalent interest cost =

$$\frac{O}{P} \times \frac{D}{T} \times 100\%$$

Where:

O = the cost of the option, in cash
P = the principal amount of the notional loan
D = the number of days in the year (money-market convention). This is 360 for most currencies, including the dollar and the euro, but 365 for some currencies such as sterling
T = the term of the notional loan period in days.

For example, suppose that a borrower's option is arranged on a notional one-year loan of £20 million and the premium is £50,000. The premium represents an effective interest cost on the loan of

$$\frac{50{,}000}{20 \text{ million}} \times \frac{365}{365} \times 100\% = 0.25\%$$

This is an approximate measure of the option's equivalent interest cost. A more accurate calculation would take account of the fact that the option is paid in advance of the start of the notional loan period, when the option is written.

Example

An organization can borrow one-year funds at sterling LIBOR plus 0.5%. It buys a borrower's option on a notional one-year loan of £20 million at a strike rate of 5.5%. The benchmark rate of interest is one-year sterling LIBOR. The premium payable is £50,000.

Analysis

By purchasing the option the organization has guaranteed for itself a maximum effective borrowing cost of 6.25%. This includes the equivalent interest cost of the option that is 0.25% (calculation above).

	%
Option strike rate	5.50
Borrowing cost over LIBOR	0.50
Premium cost	0.25
Effective borrowing cost	6.25

Outcome 1: benchmark rate at expiry higher than strike rate

Suppose that at the expiry date for the option, the one-year LIBOR rate is higher than the strike rate of 5.5% at 6.5 %.

- The organization will borrow at the current one-year LIBOR rate plus 0.5%, i.e. at 7.0 %.
- The option will be exercised, and at settlement, the option holder will receive a cash payment from the option writer for the difference in interest at the current LIBOR rate (6.5%) and the option strike rate (5.5%).

	%
Borrow at LIBOR plus 0.5%	7.00
Option settlement	- 1.00
Premium cost	0.25
Effective borrowing cost	6.25

By exercising the option, the organization has obtained its maximum guaranteed borrowing cost.

Outcome 2: benchmark rate at expiry lower than strike rate

Suppose that at the option's expiry date, the one-year LIBOR rate is lower than the option strike rate at 4.25%.

- The organization will borrow at LIBOR plus 0.5%, i.e. at 4.75%.
- The option will not be exercised.

	%
Borrow at LIBOR plus 0.5%	4.75
Premium cost	0.25
Effective borrowing cost	5.00

The borrowing cost is lower than the maximum guaranteed rate.

This example should illustrate that the cost of the option premium should be included in the overall borrowing costs when making a decision whether or not to buy a borrower's option.

Gains or Losses for the Buyer of a Borrower's Option

Before buying a borrower's option, an organization should look at the potential gains and losses that might result from the decision to buy.

Analyzing the potential gains or losses involves a comparison of

- the effective cost of borrowing if the borrower's option is purchased, and
- the cost of borrowing if the option is not purchased.

The amount of the gain or loss depends on what the benchmark rate of interest is at the option's expiry date. A range of possible outcomes can be considered.

If the effective borrowing cost with an option is less than the borrowing cost without the option, there is a gain to the option holder. If the effective borrowing cost with the option is higher than the cost of borrowing without the option, there is a loss to the option holder.

Analyzing the gains or losses for a range of possible outcomes (interest rates at expiry date) might help an organization to decide whether or not purchasing the option would be worthwhile.

Example
An organization is planning to borrow $30 million for six months, from 1 May.

The cost of the premium for a borrower's option on a notional six-month loan of $30 million would be equivalent to an annual interest cost of 0.30% on the loan. The strike rate for the option would be 6.0%. The benchmark rate of interest is the six-month dollar LIBOR rate.

For simplicity of illustration, it is assumed that the organisation can borrow funds at the six-month dollar LIBOR rate.

Analysis
The organization can assess the size of the gain or loss from a decision

to buy the option, for a range of different levels for the six-month LIBOR rate at the option's expiry date.

A range from 4.5% to 7.5%, in steps of 0.25%, is shown below.

Six-month LIBOR rate at expiry %	Effective borrowing cost with the option %	Borrowing cost with no option %	Gain or loss to the option holder %
4.50	4.80	4.50	Loss 0.30
4.75	5.05	4.75	Loss 0.30
5.00	5.30	5.00	Loss 0.30
5.25	5.55	5.25	Loss 0.30
5.50	5.80	5.50	Loss 0.30
5.75	6.05	5.75	Loss 0.30
6.00	6.30	6.00	Loss 0.30
6.25	6.30	6.25	Loss 0.05
6.50	6.30	6.50	Gain 0.20
6.75	6.30	6.75	Gain 0.45
7.00	6.30	7.00	Gain 0.70
7.25	6.30	7.25	Gain 0.95
7.50	6.30	7.50	Gain 1.20

If, at the option's expiry, the benchmark rate of interest is below the option strike rate, the option will not be exercised. The option holder will borrow at the prevailing LIBOR rate, and the effective borrowing cost, including the cost of the option, will be 0.30% higher. The loss from buying the option cannot exceed the cost of the option itself.

If, at expiry, the benchmark rate is above the strike rate in the option, the option will be exercised. The net effective borrowing cost will be capped at 6.30%, including the cost of the option. The organization will borrow at the prevailing market rate, but the option holder will receive some compensation from the option writer. If the organization did not buy the option, it would borrow at the prevailing market rate, but would not receive any compensation.

- If the compensation is less than the cost of the option, i.e. if the LIBOR rate at expiry exceeds the strike rate by less than the cost of the option (in this example, by less than 0.30%) the option holder will still make a loss, compared with what the borrowing cost would have been without the option.
- If the compensation is more than the cost of the option, i.e. if the LIBOR rate at expiry exceeds the strike rate by more than the cost of the option (in this example, by more than 0.30%) the option holder will make a profit compared with what the borrowing cost would have been without the option.

The breakeven point is the benchmark interest rate at expiry at which there would be no difference in the effective borrowing cost with or without the borrower's option. In this example, this is 6.30%. As a general rule, it is the strike rate in the option plus the cost of the option premium.

The organization can make an assessment of the probability that the six-month LIBOR rate at expiry date (start of the loan) will exceed 6.30%. If it considers the possibility sufficiently great, or the risk too high, it will choose to buy the option. If it considers the risk insufficient, it will choose not to buy the option.

The potential gains and losses for the holder of a borrower's option, using the figures in the example for illustration, can be shown on a graph, as follows:

Borrower's Option: Gain or Loss for the Holder (Buying a Call)

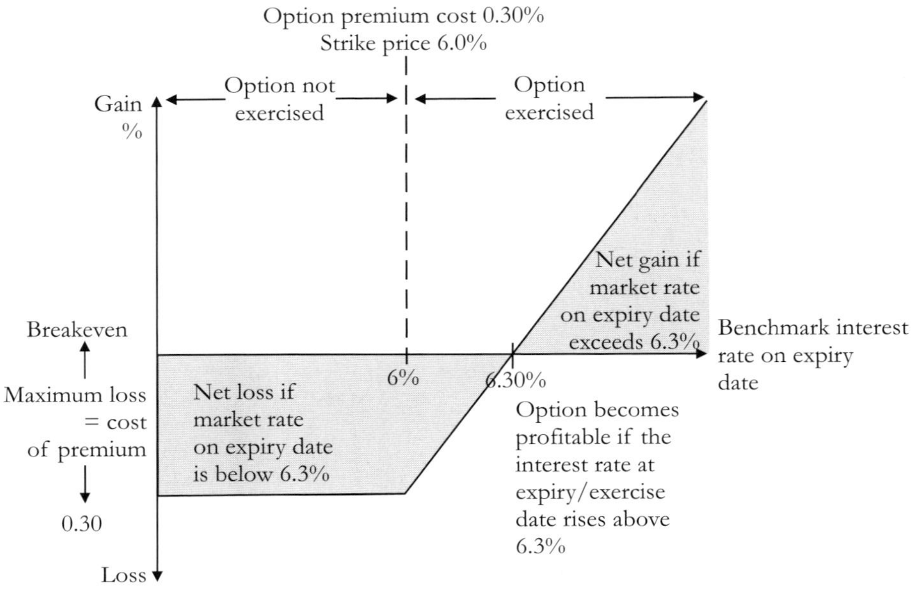

The potential gain from buying the option theoretically is limitless. In practise, the potential gain depends on how high the benchmark rate of interest might rise by the option's expiry date.

Gains or Losses for the Writer of a Borrower's Option

The position of the writer of a borrower's option is the mirror image of the option holder's position.

The option writer receives the option premium.

If at expiry the benchmark rate of interest is equal to or lower than the strike rate, the option will not be exercised. The option writer has no further obligations, and will have made a profit equal to the income from the option.

If at expiry, the benchmark rate of interest is higher than the strike rate, the option will be exercised. The option writer will make a payment to the option holder, equivalent to the difference in interest between the benchmark rate and the strike rate.

- If this difference is less than the cost of the option premium, the option writer will have made a gain overall.
- If this difference is more than the cost of the option premium, the option writer will have made a loss overall.
- The breakeven point is where the benchmark rate exceeds the strike rate by the cost of the premium. In the previous example, this is 6.30%.

The potential gains or losses for the writer of a borrower's option can be illustrated graphically as shown overleaf, using the figures in the previous example for illustration. Note in particular that

- The maximum potential gain for the option writer is the amount of the premium received.
- The potential loss theoretically is limitless, but in practise depends on how high the benchmark rate of interest might reach by the option's expiry date.
- Breakeven point, where the option writer will make neither a gain nor a loss, is when the benchmark rate at expiry equals the strike rate plus the cost of the premium.

Borrower's Option: Gain or Loss for the Writer (Writing a Call)

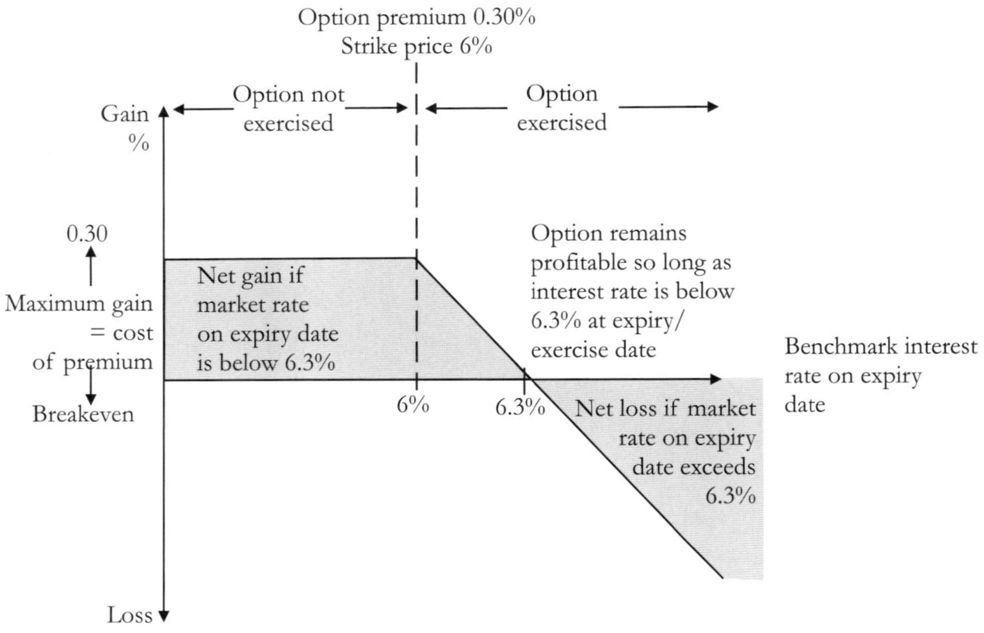

Lenders' Options

A lender's option gives its holder the right, but not the obligation, to make a notional loan for a specified principal amount and a specified term, starting at a future date (the option's expiry date) at a fixed rate of interest. This rate of interest is the option strike rate.

A lender's option can be used to guarantee a minimum rate of interest receivable on a short-term loan or on a short-term investment.

Most of the features of lenders' options are similar to those of borrowers' options. However, whereas a borrower's option is a call option on a loan, a lender's option is a put option on a loan.

- A lender's option guarantees a minimum rate of interest.
- If, at expiry, the benchmark rate of interest is lower than the option strike rate, the option will be exercised, and the option

holder will make a cash payment to the option holder for the difference between the benchmark interest rate and the option strike rate.

Lender's option

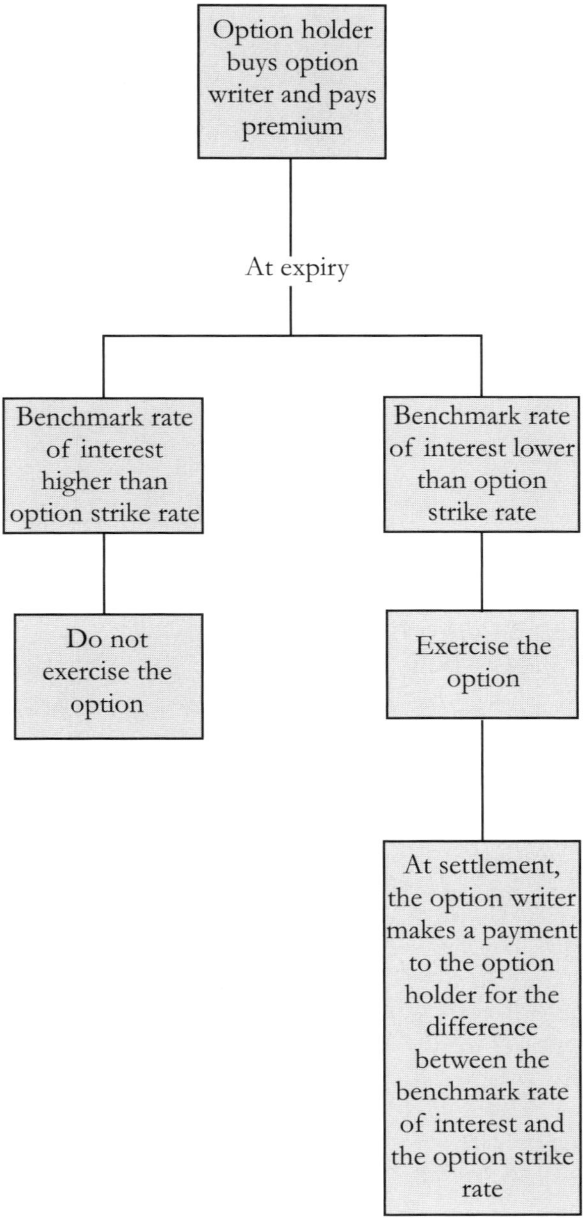

Example
An organization can lend funds at the dollar LIBOR rate plus 0.25%. It expects to have $50 million available on 15 July to lend for three months. The organization wishes to guarantee for itself a minimum rate of interest on its lending, but does not want to commit itself to a fixed rate of interest by purchasing an FRA. It wishes to buy a lender's option.

The current three-month dollar LIBOR rate is 6.0%

The organization wishes to guarantee a minimum effective rate of interest of 5.5% on its lending. Because it can lend at dollar LIBOR plus 0.25%, it wants to guarantee a minimum LIBOR rate of 5.25% *plus* an amount to cover the cost of the option premium.

It negotiates to buy a lender's option on a notional three-month loan of $50 million, with an expiry date for the option of 15 July.

- The option strike rate is 5.60%.
- The premium is $45,000 equivalent to a rate of interest of 0.35% per annum on a three-month loan of $50 million.

Analysis
At the option's expiry date, the three-month LIBOR rate could be higher or lower than the option strike rate.

Outcome 1: the benchmark rate of interest is lower than the option strike rate
Suppose, at the expiry date, the three-month LIBOR rate is lower than the option strike rate of 5.60%. Suppose it is 4.75%.

- The organization will lend $50 million at the dollar LIBOR rate plus 0.25%, i.e. at 5.0%.
- The option will be exercised, and the option writer will make a payment to the option holder for the 0.85% difference between the three-month LIBOR rate (4.75%) and the option strike rate (5.60%).

The effective interest income for the organization for the three-month lending will be:

	%
Interest on lending	5.00
Compensation received	0.85
Cost of option premium	- 0.35
Net effective interest income	5.50

Outcome 2: the benchmark rate of interest is higher than the option strike rate
Suppose, at the expiry date, the three-month LIBOR rate is higher than the option strike rate of 5.60%. Suppose it is 6.0 %.

- The organization will lend $50 million at the dollar LIBOR rate plus 0.25%, i.e. at 6.25%.
- The option will not be exercised.

The effective interest income for the organization for the three-month lending will be:

	%
Interest on lending	6.25
Cost of option premium	- 0.35
Net effective interest income	5.90

This example should illustrate that lenders' options can be used to guarantee a minimum rate of interest income, from lending or investing, but also allow the option holder to benefit from a more favorable interest rate at the option's expiry date. This is because exercising the option is at the holder's choice, and is not obligatory.

However, lenders' options have a cost that effectively reduces the minimum effective rate of interest receivable.

Gains or Losses for the Holder and Writer of a Lender's Option

The position for the holder of a lender's option can be compared with what the position would be if there were no option. Analyzing an option holder's potential gains or losses is similar to the analysis for a borrower's option, described earlier. Making this sort of analysis might help an organization to judge whether or not to buy the option.

An analysis also can be made of the option writer's gains or losses.

Example

An organization can deposit short-term funds for one year at the euribor rate. It expects to have €25 million to invest for one year, and is considering the purchase of a lender's option to guarantee a minimum investment yield because it has some concerns about the possibility of an imminent fall in the euribor rate.

The current one-year euribor rate is 5.0% and the organization wants to secure a minimum effective investment yield of 4.75%.

A lender's option on €25 million for one year at a strike rate of 4.90% would have a premium cost of €37,000. This premium would be equivalent to an annual interest cost of 0.15% on a loan of €25 million for one year.

Analysis

The lender's option would secure a minimum guaranteed investment yield for the organization of 4.75%.

	%
Minimum investment yield guaranteed by strike rate	4.90
Cost of option premium	- 0.15
Net effective interest income	4.75

The potential gains or losses for the option holder and the option writer are shown in the following table, for a range of possible values for the euribor rate at the option's expiry.

Euribor rate at expiry of option %	Effective investment yield with the option %	Investment yield with no option %	Gain or loss to the option holder %	Option premium received %	Payment to option holder on exercise of option %	Gain or loss to option holder %
3.50	4.75	3.50	Gain 1.25	0.15	1.40	Loss 1.25
3.75	4.75	3.75	Gain 1.00	0.15	1.15	Loss 1.00
4.00	4.75	4.00	Gain 0.75	0.15	0.90	Loss 0.75
4.25	4.75	4.25	Gain 0.50	0.15	0.65	Loss 0.50
4.50	4.75	4.50	Gain 0.25	0.15	0.40	Loss 0.25
4.75	4.75	4.75	Breakeven	0.15	0.15	Breakeven
5.00	4.85	5.00	Loss 0.15	0.15	0	Gain 0.15
5.25	5.10	5.25	Loss 0.15	0.15	0	Gain 0.15
5.50	5.35	5.50	Loss 0.15	0.15	0	Gain 0.15
5.75	5.60	5.75	Loss 0.15	0.15	0	Gain 0.15
6.00	5.85	6.00	Loss 0.15	0.15	0	Gain 0.15
6.25	6.10	6.25	Loss 0.15	0.15	0	Gain 0.15
6.50	6.35	6.50	Loss 0.15	0.15	0	Gain 0.15

Notes on the table

- The option will be exercised if the euribor rate at expiry is lower than the option strike rate of 4.90%. The compensation payable by the option writer to the option holder is the difference between the euribor rate at expiry and the strike rate. After deducting the cost of the premium, the effective investment income to the option holder, when the option is exercised, is 4.75%
- Without the option, the option holder would invest at the euribor rate.
- The maximum loss for the option holder is 0.15%, the cost of the option premium.

The position for the option holder is the mirror image of the position for the option writer. The gain for one is matched by an equal loss for the other.

The potential gains and losses for the option holder and option writer can be illustrated graphically, as follows.

Lender's Option: Gain or Loss for the Holder (Buying a Put)

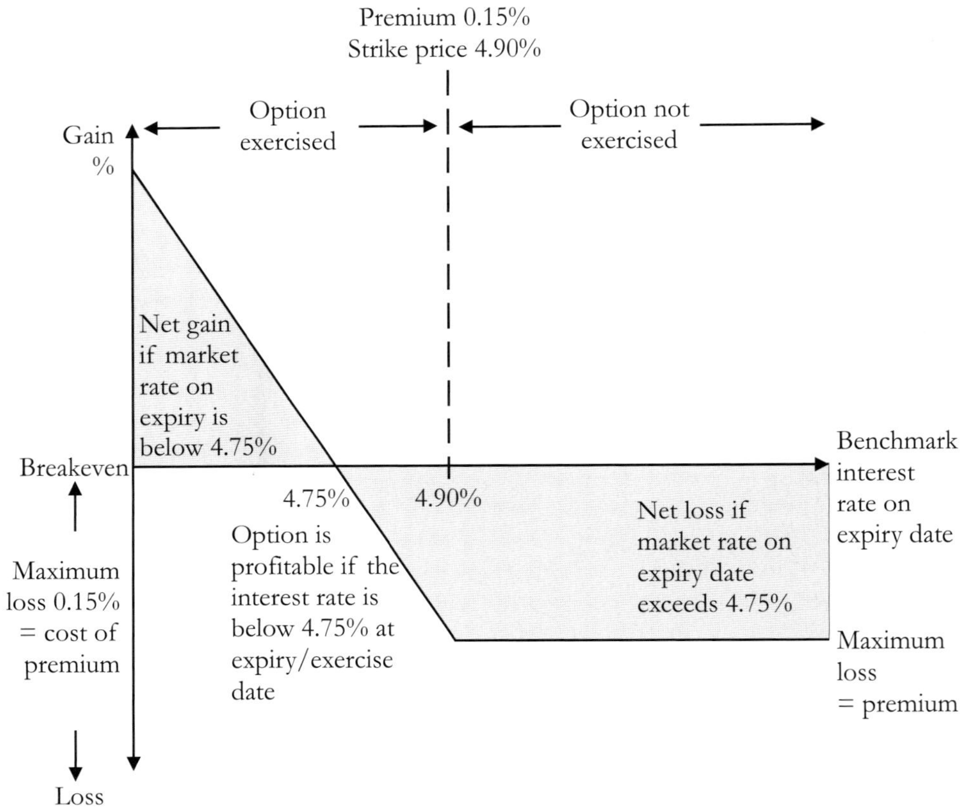

Lender's Option: Gain or Loss for the Writer (Writing a Put)

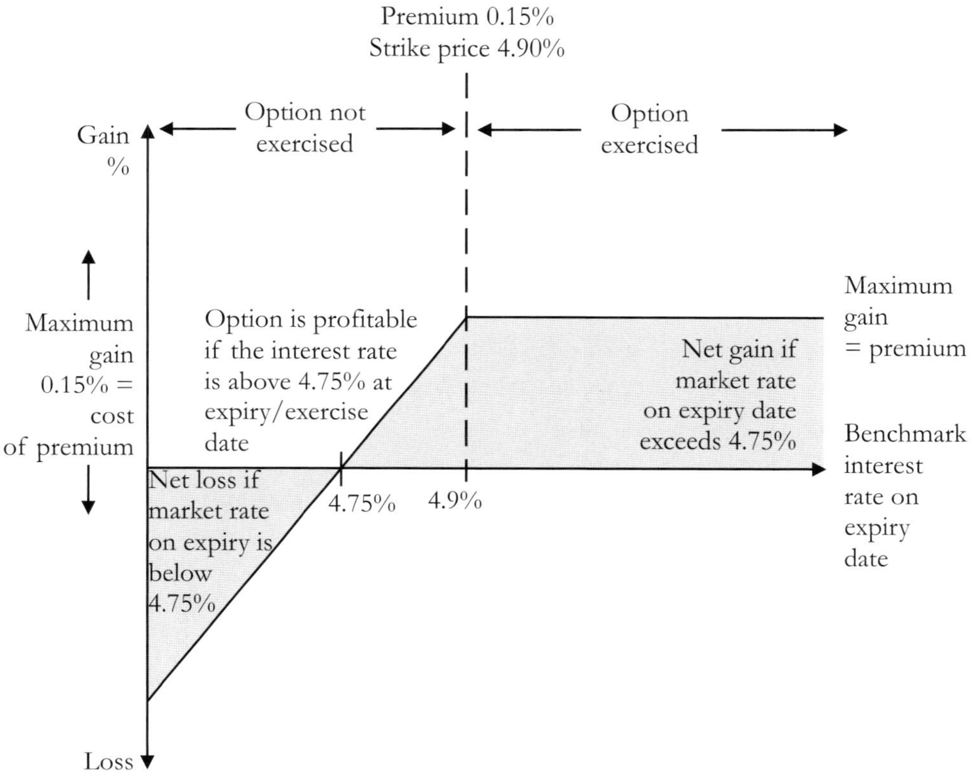

Gains and Losses as a Zero-Sum Game

The gain or loss for the option holder is always matched by an equal loss or gain for the option writer. The gain or loss for the option holder plus the loss or gain for the option writer must always add up to zero. The option holder and option writer therefore are in a zero-sum game where one party can make a profit only at the expense of the other.

It would be reasonable to assume that in the long run, professional option writers will make profits at the expense of their clients, the option buyers. Clients that buy options to hedge an interest-rate risk should expect to incur some costs for the interest-rate insurance that the option provides.

Ultimately, the size of gains or losses will depend on the amount paid for the option premiums. Option prices are derived from mathematical models, and pricing is considered in some detail in a later chapter.

Buyers' and Lenders' Options: Selecting a Strike Rate

Buyers' and lenders' options are OTC instruments, and the terms of the agreement are subject to negotiation. An option buyer can think about what strike rate would be most appropriate, and compare different strike rates. Strike rates that are more favorable to the option buyer obviously cost more.

Example
An organization is expecting to borrow £20 million for six months in the near future. The interest rate for sterling is expected to remain reasonably stable, but the organization nevertheless wants to guarantee a maximum borrowing cost in the event of a rise in the interest level.

A bank is offering two borrower's option arrangements.

- An option with a strike rate of 6.5%. The option premium would have an interest cost equivalent of 0.4 %.
- An option with a strike rate of 7.0 %. The option premium would have an interest cost equivalent of 0.15 %.

It will be assumed that the organization can borrow at the six-month sterling LIBOR rate.

Analysis

	Strike rate 6.5% %	Strike rate 7.0% %
Premium cost = maximum possible loss	0.40	0.15
Effective maximum borrowing cost	6.90	7.15
Breakeven point for losses	6.90	7.15

The choice facing the organization is whether to pay a smaller premium for a higher maximum borrowing cost, or to pay more for a lower guaranteed maximum cost.

Using Borrowers' and Lenders' Options

Borrowers' and lenders' options are used

- to hedge exposures to interest-rate risk
- to speculate in interest-rate movements.

As hedging instruments, borrowers' options are used to guarantee a maximum borrowing cost and lenders' options are used to guarantee a minimum interest yield on lending or investing. Examples of using options for these purposes have been given previously.

Borrowers' and lenders' options also can be used to speculate on future interest-rate movements. The underlying item is a notional loan, not an actual loan, and the option holder is in no way committed to obtaining or making a loan.

The option buyer incurs the cost of the premium, and will hope to make an overall gain from exercising the option. An option writer sells an option and hopes to make a profit in the event that the option is not exercised. The potential gains or losses for a speculator either buying or writing options have been illustrated earlier.

A number of option strategies for traders or speculators in interest-rate options are described in a later chapter.

Limitations of Borrowers' and Lenders' Options

Borrowers' and lenders' options have some limitations.

- They can be expensive to buy, particularly when interest rates are volatile.
- When interest rates are fairly stable, the scale of a borrower's or lender's exposure to interest-rate risk will be much less than when interest rates are uncertain and volatile. The opportunities to profit from speculating on interest-rate movements also will be fewer. Interest-rate options, like other derivative instruments, are in greater demand when perceived risks are greater.

3

Settlement of Borrowers' and Lenders' Options

Cash Settlement: Settlement for Difference

A borrower's option is a call option on a notional loan, rather than an actual loan, and a lender's option is a put on a notional deposit. When a borrower's option or a lender's option is exercised, the option holder and option writer do not arrange an actual loan or deposit. Instead, there is a cash settlement, and the option writer makes a payment to the option holder. The amount of the cash payment represents a difference in interest on the notional loan between interest at the benchmark rate and interest at the option strike rate.

If settlement took place at the **end** of the notional loan period, the amount of the cash payment would be calculated by the following formula.

$$P \times \frac{(B - S)}{100} \times \frac{T}{D}$$

where:

- P is the notional principal amount.
- B is the benchmark rate of interest (7% = 7, 4.35% = 4.35, etc.)
- S is the option strike rate (8.5% = 8.5, 6.75% = 6.75, etc.)
- (B – S) therefore is the difference between the benchmark rate and the option strike rate. It cannot be a negative amount.
- T is the length of the notional loan period, in days
- D is the days convention in the money markets, and is the

number of days in a full year, for interest purposes. For most currencies, including the dollar and the euro, D is 360. For some currencies, including sterling, D is 365.

Example

An organisation buys a borrower's option on a notional one-year (365 day) loan of $10 million. The strike rate is 6.0%. At expiry date for the option, the benchmark one-year interest rate is 7.5%.

The option will be exercised. *If settlement were to take place at the end of the notional loan period*, i.e. one year after the option's expiry date, the amount of the cash settlement, payable by the option writer, would be:

$$\$10,000,000 \times \frac{(7.5 - 6.0)}{100} \times \frac{365}{360} = \$152,083.33$$

The Timing of the Cash Settlement

Settlement of a borrower's or lender's option usually takes place at the expiry date of the option, one or two business days after the holder has notified the writer of his intention to exercise the option. The option's expiry date is at the beginning of the notional loan period to which the option relates.

Borrowers' and lenders' options are over-the-counter instruments that means the settlement date is negotiable. Settlement could be arranged, for example, to take place on the last day of the notional loan period. However, settlement at the option exercise date is normal.

When settlement takes place at the option exercise date, the option holder is receiving interest for the full notional loan period when the period is only just beginning. The amount of the payment therefore should be reduced. The interest that would be payable at the end of the loan period should be discounted to a present value as at the start of the loan period.

The Settlement Amount: Settlement at the Option Exercise Date

When settlement takes place at the option exercise date, the start of the notional loan or deposit period, the amount of the settlement can be calculated using the formula:

$$\text{Settlement} = P \times \frac{(B - S)}{100} \times \frac{T}{D} \times \left[\frac{1}{1 + \left(\frac{B \times T}{100 \times D} \right)} \right]$$

The final element in the formula is a discount factor, to reduce the terminal value or end-of-loan period interest payment to a start-of-loan-period present value. This formula can be re-arranged into a simpler form:

$$\text{Settlement} = \frac{P \times (B - S) \times T}{[(D \times 100) + (B \times T)]}$$

The discounted amount assumes that the option holder could invest the payment received for the duration of the notional loan period to earn interest at the benchmark rate.

Example 1

An organization buys a borrower's option on a notional six-month loan (183 days) of €20 million. The strike rate is 4.5%.

At the option's expiry date, suppose the benchmark six-month interest rate is 5.3%. The option will be exercised, and at settlement on the expiry date, the payment from the option writer to the option holder will be:

$$\text{Settlement in euros} = \frac{20 \text{ million} \times (5.3 - 4.5) \times 183}{[(360 \times 100) + (5.3 \times 183)]}$$

$$= €79{,}199.57$$

Example 2
An organization buys a lender's option on a notional three-month loan (91 days) of £15 million. The strike rate is 6.0%.

At the option's expiry, suppose the benchmark three-month interest rate is 4.8%. The option will be exercised. If settlement takes place on the expiry date, the amount of the payment will be:

$$\text{Settlement} = \frac{£15 \text{ million} \times (6.0 - 4.8) \times 91}{[(365 \times 100) + (4.8 \times 91)]}$$

$= £44,346.02$

The Effective Borrowing or Lending Rate

The effective borrowing rate for a call-option holder or lending rate for a put-option holder is not the strike price of the option for two reasons.

- The holder of a borrower's option cannot borrow at LIBOR but will have to pay a margin above LIBOR. Similarly, the holder of a lender's option might deposit funds only at a margin below LIBOR.
- The cost of the option premium also should be taken into account when calculating the effective overall cost of borrowing or the overall return on lending.

It is useful to look at an example, even though the mathematics might seem complex.

Example
A company has a money-market investment of £10 million on which it receives interest twice a year at 100 basis points below LIBOR (LIBOR minus 1% p.a.). It buys a lender's option for expiry to coincide with the next rollover date for the investment interest at a strike price of 7%. For simplicity, the cost of the option premium will be ignored.

Analysis

On expiry date, if six-month LIBOR is above the strike price at 7.75%, the company will let the option lapse and the investment for the next six months will earn interest at 6.75% (LIBOR minus 1%).

If however, on expiry date LIBOR is below the strike price at for example, 9.5%, the put option will be exercised. The company will earn interest at 8.5% (LIBOR minus 1%) on its investment for the next six months, but the cash settlement payment from the option writer will increase the effective interest rate by 0.5%, the difference between the strike price and LIBOR. The option holder's overall return therefore will be the strike price minus 1%.

	%
Investment yield (LIBOR minus 1%)	5.0
Cash settlement	1.5
Overall yield	6.5

The cash settlement will be as follows:

$$\frac{£10 \text{ million} \times (7.5 - 6.0) \times 182}{(365 \times 100) + (6.0 \times 182)} = £72,622$$

If the £10 million principal plus the cash settlement from exercising the option is invested for the next six months at LIBOR minus 100 basis points, the value of the investment at the end of the period will be:

$$£10,072,622 \times \left[1 + \left(\frac{182}{365} \times \frac{5.0}{100}\right)\right] = £10,323,747$$

This represents a total return of £323,747 on the £10 million investment over the one-year period. This gives an effective return on investment of

$$\frac{323,747}{10 \text{ million}} \times \frac{365}{183} = 6.5\%$$

Exercise

A company has a floating rate loan of $20 million for which it pays six-month dollar LIBOR + 1.5%. It has purchased a borrower's option on six-month dollar LIBOR at 6.5%. What will be the company's effective borrowing rate if six-month dollar LIBOR on the expiry date is:

(a) 5.5%?
(b) 6.5%?
(c) 7.0%?
(d) 9.0%?

Ignore the cost of the premium.

How much, if anything, will the cash settlement by the option writer be, assuming a 183-day loan period?

Solution

(a) The option will not be exercised. Funds will be borrowed at LIBOR + 1.5% for the next six months. This will be a rate of 7% (5.5+1.5).

(b) The option will not be exercised because the strike price equals LIBOR. Funds will be borrowed at LIBOR + 1.5% for the next six months. This will be a rate of 8% (6.5 + 1.5).

(c) The option will be exercised. Funds will be borrowed at LIBOR + 1.5% for the next six months. This rate is 8.5% (7+ 1.5). However, the cash settlement from the bank will reduce the effective interest rate to 8% (6.5 + 1.5) because this payment is worth 0.5% (the difference between LIBOR and the strike price).

The payment will be

$$\frac{\$20 \text{ million} \times (6.5 - 7.0) \times 183}{(360 \times 100) + (7.0 \times 183)} = \$49{,}087$$

(d) The option will be exercised. Funds will be borrowed at 10.5% but the cash settlement from the bank will reduce the effective interest rate to 8% (6.5+ 1.5).
If six-month LIBOR is 9.0% and there are 183 days in the six-month period, the cash settlement will be

$$\frac{\$20 \text{ million} \times (6.5 - 9.0) \times 183}{(360 \times 100) + (9.0 \times 183)} = \$243{,}047$$

In situation (d) the net cost of interest for the option user for the six-month period will be

	$
Interest on borrowed funds at 10.5%	1,067,500
($20 million x 10.5% x 183/360)	
Less cash settlement received	(243,047)
Net cost of interest for six months	824,453

Allowing for the fact that the cash settlement will be received at the start of the loan period, and the interest will be payable at the end of the period, this net interest cost will represent an annual interest cost on the $20 million borrowing of 8% per annum.

4

Interest-Rate Caps, Floors and Collars

Interest-rate caps, floors and collars are types of OTC interest rate options. Whereas borrowers' or lenders' options are essentially short-term instruments relating to one notional loan or deposit period, caps, floors and collars are long-term instruments. Caps, floors and collars might be used by borrowers with medium-term floating rate loans or lenders with medium-term variable rate deposits, as a means of fixing their loan costs or investment yields.

Interest-Rate Caps

An interest-rate cap is a series of borrowers' options that sets a maximum interest-rate cost for medium-term floating-rate borrowing. The buyer of a cap can choose the strike rate required, thereby fixing a maximum borrowing rate, but the cost of the premium will vary with the strike rate chosen. The cap holder has the right to exercise an option on each fixing date or rollover date of the loan, and this covers the interest period up to the next fixing date. In practise, however, no formal notice of exercise is necessary – unlike a borrower's option. If, on any fixing date, the market rate of interest is above the cap's strike price, exercise and cash settlement are triggered automatically.

Example

A company might obtain a two-year floating-rate loan of £10 million with interest payable six-monthly at LIBOR plus 1%, on 30 June and 31 December in each of Year 1 and Year 2. Six-month LIBOR is currently 5.5%, but the company is concerned about the risk of a significant increase in interest rates within the next few months. The company might decide to hedge the risk and buy an interest-rate cap, setting a limit of, for example, 6% p.a. to six-month LIBOR. The cap would consist of a series of three call options on six-month LIBOR for a notional principal of £10 million at a strike price of 6% p.a. for each option. The expiry dates for each option would coincide with the interest rollover dates that in this example would be

Expiry date	To cover the period
30 June Year 1	1 July Year 1-31 December Year 1
31 December Year 1	1 January Year 2-30 June Year 2
30 June Year 2	1 July Year 2-31 December Year 2 (end of the loan period).

Interest-Rate Caps: Option Exercise Dates

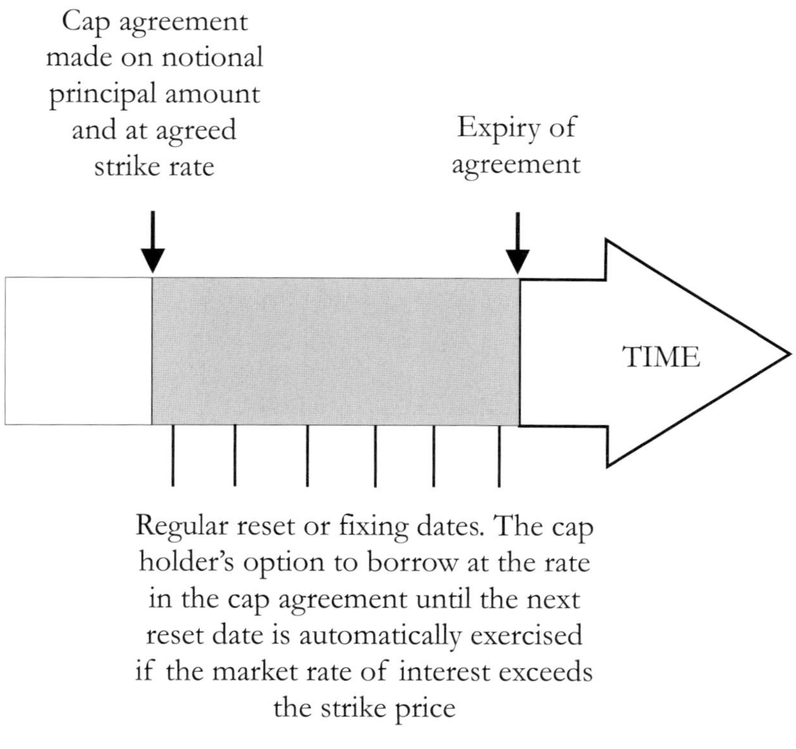

Interest-Rate Caps: Option Exercise Dates

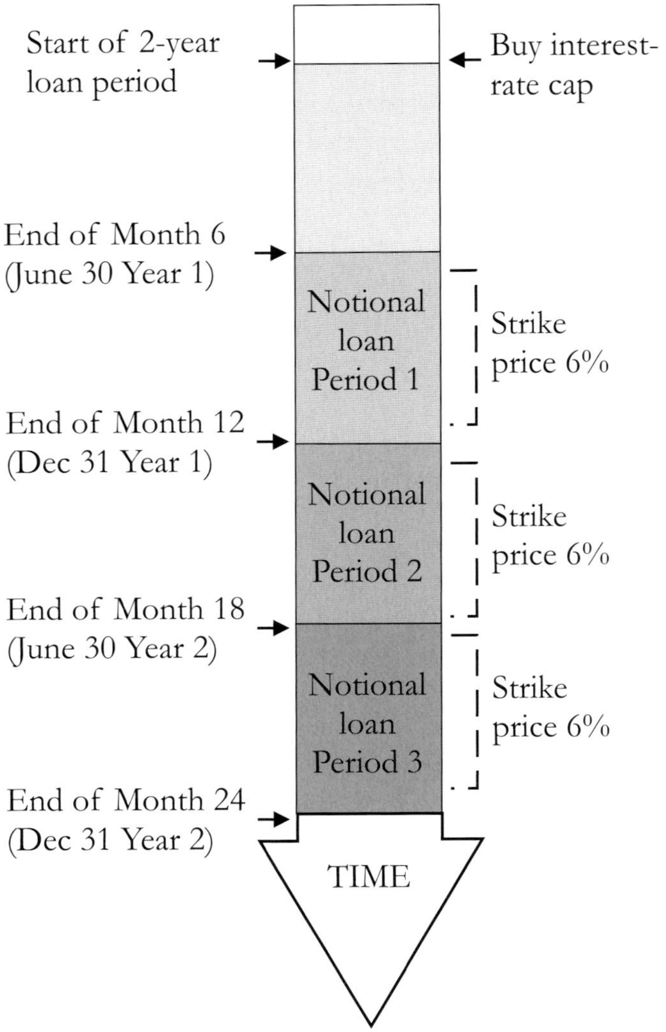

The cap is a series of three borrower's options, each for a six-month loan period at a strike price of 6%. The cap therefore can be described as an option on three forward-rate agreements (FRAs):

- a 6 v 12 FRA (fixed rate 6%)
- a 12 v 18 FRA (fixed rate 6%)
- an 18 v 24 FRA (fixed rate 6%).

Caps can be written for periods as short as three months, making them much the same as a borrower's option, and up to 12 years. Most caps are for periods of between two and five years. They were devised in the mid-1980s to accompany the issue of floating-rate notes to protect the issuer of the notes (the borrower) against rising interest rates over the term to maturity of the notes.

Like borrowers' options, caps are cash-settled. The cap writer (seller) pays a compensating amount to the cap holder when the interest rate is above the pre-agreed strike level on the expiry date for any of the options in the series. However, unlike borrowers' options, the settlement of caps usually is at the *end* of the notional loan period, not at the beginning of the period.

Example

A company has $20 million of outstanding debt at floating-rate interest of dollar LIBOR plus 1%, with a maturity of four years and rollover dates every three months. It is worried about interest rates rising in the next four years, increasing the cost of borrowing, and does not want to pay more than 8% interest. It therefore buys a cap on three-month LIBOR with a strike price of 7%. The terms are

Strike level	7%
Underlying index	Three-month dollar LIBOR
Notional principal amount	$20 million
Maturity	Four years
Frequency of reset dates	Three months

Analysis

Every three months interest on the actual loan is reset at 100 basis points above the current three-month LIBOR rate. If actual LIBOR is higher than 7% at a reset date, the company will receive a compensating amount from the cap writer (the bank) for the difference between LIBOR and the strike level of 7%, for the period until the next reset date that in this example is for the next three months.

If LIBOR is below 7% on the reset date, the option will not be exercised and the company simply will pay interest on its loan at LIBOR +1% for the next three months.

A cap therefore guarantees that the maximum net cost of borrowing for the four-year period will be 8% (the strike level of 7% plus 100 basis points). The company is guaranteed against an increase in interest rates above the strike level but can also benefit from lower interest rates.

The table below shows what would occur if three-month LIBOR were as shown on each reset date.

Strike rate 7% Reset date (end of)	**3-month LIBOR (%)**	**Compensation payment?**
Month 3 Year 1	6.5	No
Month 6 Year 1	6.0	No
Month 9 Year 1	5.75	No
Month 12 Year 1	6.25	No
Month 3 Year 2	6.75	No
Month 6 Year 2	7.5	Yes (0.5%)
Month 9 Year 2	7.5	Yes (0.5%)
Month 12 Year 2	8.5	Yes (1.5%)
Month 3 Year 3	9.0	Yes (2.0%)
Month 6 Year 3	9.5	Yes (2.5%)
Month 9 Year 3	8.5	Yes (1.5%)
Month 12 Year 3	8.5	Yes (1.5%)
Month 3 Year 4	8.5	Yes (1.5%)
Month 6 Year 4	7.0	No
Month 9 Year 4	5.5	No

Features of Interest-Rate Caps

The features of interest-rate caps are similar in many respects to borrowers' options.

- *Strike level.* The strike level or strike price of a cap is the maximum (guaranteed) interest rate. It is usually a *whole number* percentage figure, 5%, 6%, 7%, 8%, 9% etc, because it tends to be a threshold figure for LIBOR beyond which companies do not wish their cost of funds to rise.

- *Underlying index.* The underlying index is the reference interest rate to which the strike level applies. Caps typically are written on three-month LIBOR or six-month LIBOR, but another reference rate used for pricing variable rate borrowing, such as one-month LIBOR, a Treasury Bill rate or a commercial paper rate, might be used.
- *Notional principal amount.* As with borrowers' options, there is a notional principal amount for the cap, on which any compensating amounts payable by the cap writer (seller) are based. The notional principal amount for a cap is unlikely to be less than about $10 million and could be much higher. Where a borrower is gradually repaying loan principal over time, the notional principal amount for a cap can be amortized as the outstanding loan principal is repaid in order to preserve an exact match.
- *Currency.* Caps are written in all the major trading currencies.
- *Maturity.* Cap maturities typically are two to five years. They can be up to about 12 years or as short as three months.
- *Reset dates.* The review dates, when compensating amounts are payable by the cap writer, should coincide with rollover dates for the underlying borrowings of the cap buyer. These reset dates that are also called fixing dates, are typically every six months, three months or one month.
- *Premium.* This is a front-end fee paid as soon as the cap is written. It is quoted in basis points (hundredths of 1%) on the notional principal. Premiums typically are between 100 and 500 basis points (1% - 5% of the notional principal amount).

Because caps are OTC instruments, their details are negotiated individually between customer and bank. Reset dates, for example, can be set to the customer's specific requirements to match rollover dates on an underlying loan; and the underlying index will be the same reference rate as for the loan itself.

Cash Settlements: Interest-Rate Caps

When the reference interest rate (underlying index) exceeds the strike level on a reset date for the cap, the cap writer pays the cap holder a compensating amount.

The compensating amount usually is paid in *arrears*. For example, on a cap with quarterly reset dates, the cap writer will make any compensating payment *three months after the reset date*. In this respect, caps differ from most borrowers' option agreements, where the settlement amount is paid up front.

Because settlement is at the end of the notional loan period, there is no need to discount to present value the amount of the payment to the cap holder. The following formula is used to calculate the compensating amount payable when the underlying index exceeds the strike rate on the reset date

$$\frac{(L - R) \times D \times P}{Y \times 100}$$

Where

- L is the underlying index, for example three-month LIBOR or six-month LIBOR
- R is the strike rate
- D is the number of days in the interest period until the next reset date
- P is the notional principal amount
- Y is the assumed number of days in the year for the purpose of calculating interest. The value of Y is 365 for some currencies, including sterling. It is 360 for most currencies, including the dollar and the euro.

Example 1

A company has an interest-rate cap on a notional principal amount of $30 million. The underlying index is three-month LIBOR and the strike level is 6%.

At a reset date on 31 May Year 1, three-month LIBOR is 7%. The next interest-rate period is 92 days.

Analysis
On 31 May Year 1, the cap holder will exercise the option and a compensating amount will be agreed by the cap writer. This amount will be

$$\frac{(7 - 6) \times 92 \times \$30 \text{ million}}{360 \times 100}$$

$$= \$76{,}667$$

This compensating amount will be paid to the cap holder on the next reset date which is 31 August Year 1.

Example 2
A company has variable-rate borrowings of £20 million that are repayable in full in two years' time and roll over every six months. Interest on the loan is at LIBOR plus 50 basis points. Six-month LIBOR is currently 6%. The company wishes to set a maximum cost of 7.5% on its borrowings and buys an interest-rate cap from its bank. The terms are

Strike level	7%
Underlying index	Six-month LIBOR
Notional principal amount	£20 million
Maturity	Two years
Reset dates	Every six months
Premium	100 basis points

The cap is arranged on 31 December Year 0, and six-month LIBOR on the reset dates are

30 June Year 1	8.5%
31 December Year 1	6.5%
30 June Year 2	8.0%

The interest period is

31 December - 30 June	181 days
1 July - 31 December	184 days

Analysis

Under the terms of the agreement, the writer of the cap must pay the holder compensation for any six-month period when LIBOR is above 7%. If LIBOR is below 7% on the fixing date no payment is made. This is illustrated below:

Cap: Compensating Payments

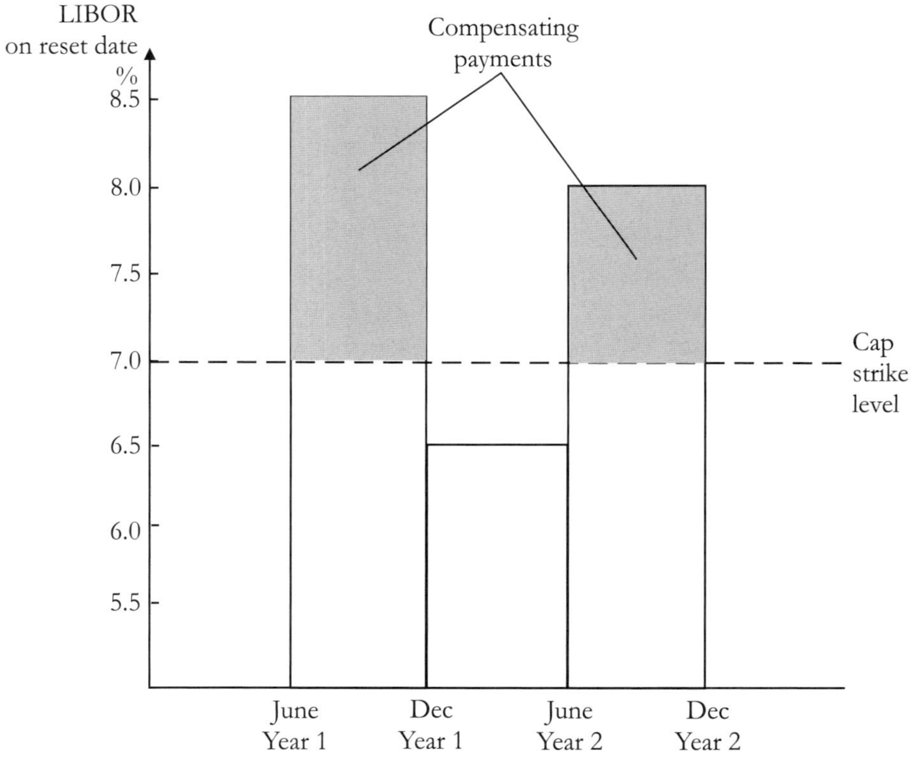

The shaded area indicates the amount of compensation that the cap holder will receive. The cap writer will make payments on December Year 1 for the period July-December Year 1 and in December Year 2 for the period July to December Year 2. Because LIBOR was below the strike level in December Year 1, there is no compensating payment for the period January to June Year 2.

Cash flows under the cap agreement will be

31 December Year 0 (or soon after)	£
Premium payable is 1% of £20 million	(200,000)
In the period 31 December Year 0-30 June Year 1, the company pays LIBOR + 0.5% = 10.5% on its loan	

30 June Year 1

LIBOR exceeds strike level.

Compensating payment =

$$\frac{(8.5 - 7) \times 184 \times 320 \text{ million}}{365 \times 100}$$

Compensating payment paid in arrears, on 31 December Year 1	£151,233

Interest on loan, 30 June-31 December Year 1 is LIBOR + 0.5 = 8.5% + 0.50% = 9%

31 December Year 1

LIBOR at 31 December Year 1 is below the strike level, therefore the option (cap) is not exercised at this reset date. Interest on the £20 million loan is set at LIBOR plus 0.5% = 6.5% + 0.50% = 7%, for the period 31 December-30 June Year 2

30 June Year 2

LIBOR exceeds strike level.

Compensating payment =

$$\frac{(8 - 7) \times 184 \times \pounds 20 \text{ million}}{365 \times 100}$$

Compensating payment is paid at the end of the six-month notional loan period, on 31 December Year 2	£100,822

Interest on loan, 30 June-31 December Year 2
is LIBOR + 0.5% = 8% + 0.5% = 8.5%.

The compensating payments on 31 December in Year 1 and 31 December Year 2 have capped the borrowing costs at 0.5% above the cap strike level of 7%.

	Period 30 June-31 Dec Year 1	**Period 30 June-31 Dec Year 2**
Interest rate on loan	9%	8.5%
	£	£
Interest on loan (184 days)	907,397	856,986
Compensating amount	(151,233)	(100,822)
Net interest cost	756,164	756,164

Interest costs of £756,164 for 184 days on a loan of £20 million represents an annual interest rate of 7.5%.

In the six-month period 1 January to 30 June Year 2, the interest rate payable is 7%, and so ignoring the £200,000 cost of the cap premium, the cost of borrowing for the two-year period has been kept below 7.5%.

Advantages and Disadvantages of Caps

The advantages of interest-rate caps are that they

- enable the holder to set a maximum fixed rate for floating-rate funds and therefore a maximum cost for borrowing, and also
- allow the holder to benefit from any fall in interest rates below the strike level.

Therefore they can provide an attractive method of hedging an exposure to interest-rate risk on floating-rate borrowings over the medium term.

The main disadvantages of caps is their high cost. The option writer is taking on a medium-term interest-rate risk from the cap buyer, and will charge a premium accordingly.

How Caps are Used

Caps originated in the mid-1980s as an extension of the interest-rate option market. They are used by companies in a number of ways.

- Risk-averse companies with variable rate medium-term borrowings can buy a cap to hedge against increases in interest rates when they finance a major takeover with floating-rate borrowing. When a company purchases another company for cash, and borrows at a variable rate to finance the purchase, it is exposed to the risk of an increase in interest rates unless and until the variable-rate loans can be replaced by fixed-rate finance (bonds) or equity finance. For the cost of the cap premium a company can set a maximum financing cost on the acquisition for several years if required, and reduce significantly its interest-rate risk.
- Property companies funding development projects with variable-rate loans can use a cap to set a maximum limit on the interest cost of the project. The cap therefore helps ensure a project is profitable.
- A management buyout (MBO) or leveraged buyout (LBO) may be financed by medium-term variable-rate loans. Caps can be used to place a maximum level on funding costs for some or all of the debt because highly leveraged companies are more vulnerable to interest-rate increases than modestly geared companies. This secures a downside maximum cost to the funding.

Captions

A caption is an option to buy a cap at some date in the future. It might be used by an organization that is uncertain about the future need for a cap, perhaps because it is unsure about whether or not it will need to raise a large floating-rate loan at some time in the future. If the loan is obtained, however, the organization probably would wish to purchase a cap. Purchasing a caption would enable it to

- set interest rates (the strike level) now for the future cap
- let the caption lapse, either if interest rates move in the company's favor before the date the cap is needed, or if the cap is not required.

Interest-Rate Floors

Whereas an interest-rate cap is a series of interest-rate call options (borrowers' options), an interest-rate floor is a series of interest-rate put options (lenders' options). A floor therefore can be used to hedge against the risk of falling interest rates for medium-term floating-rate lending or for investing at variable interest rates. Interest-rate floors thus provide a minimum guaranteed interest rate for the income of a lender or investor.

On each reset date during the period of the agreement, the holder's right to lend or invest the notional principal at the strike rate can be exercised for the period to the next reset date. Exercise will be automatic if the strike price is higher than the reference market rate of interest.

Interest-Rate Floors: Option Exercise Date

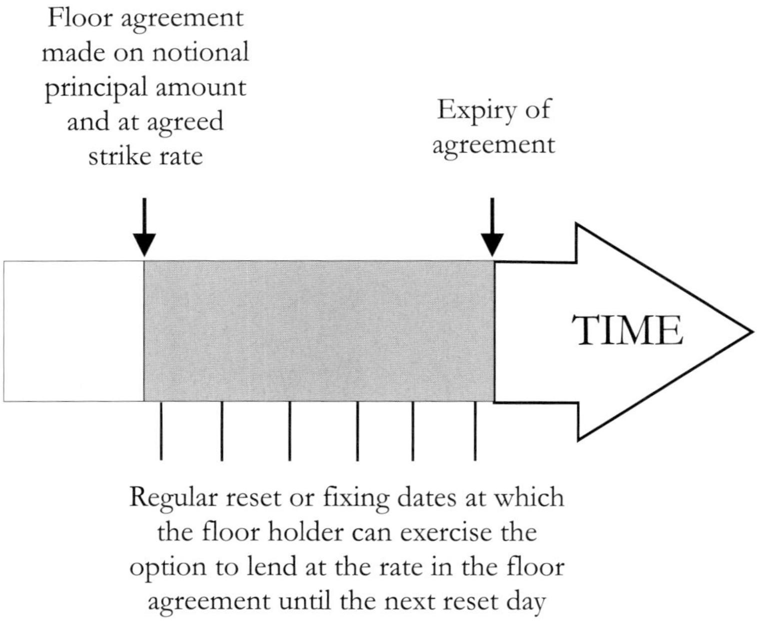

An interest-rate floor is similar in most respects to a cap in the same way that a lender's option is similar to a borrower's option.

If the market interest rate is below the strike level on a reset date, a compensating amount is calculated and subsequently paid in arrears at the next reset date. This amount is calculated from the following formula that is similar to the formula for the compensating amount with an interest-rate cap.

$$\frac{(R - L) \times D \times P}{Y \times 100}$$

Where

- R is the strike rate
- L is the underlying index, three-month LIBOR, six-month LIBOR, etc.
- D is the number of days in the interest period until the next reset date
- P is the notional principal amount
- Y is the assumed number of days in the year for the purpose of calculating interest. The value of Y is 365 for some currencies, including sterling. It is 360 for most currencies, including the dollar and the euro.

If interest rates are above the strike level on the reset date, the lender/investor will choose not to exercise his option under the floor agreement, and will simply lend or invest at the market rate of interest.

Example
A cash-rich company has invested £25 million in floating-rate notes (FRNs) that pay interest of six-month LIBOR plus 100 basis points. Six-month LIBOR is currently 6.5%. The company is partly financed by fixed-rate funds paying 7%, and wants to be sure that income from its FRNs will at least cover the cost of its debt obligations. It therefore wants to guarantee that the income from its investments will not fall below a minimum of 7%.

It buys an interest-rate floor with a strike level at 6%, based on an underlying index of six-month LIBOR. The maturity of the floor matches the period for which the company expects to hold the FRN investment, in this case three years. Reset dates for the floor coincide with the six-monthly rollover dates (fixing dates) for the FRN.

The premium payable for the floor is 225 basis points. At the reset dates for the floor, six-month LIBOR is

Reset date	LIBOR %	Floor
1	7.0	Out-of-the-money
2	6.5	Out-of-the-money
3	5.0	In-the-money
4	6.0	At-the-money
5	4.0	In-the-money

Analysis
The cost of the floor premium is £562,500 (2.25% x £25 million)

The floor writer (the bank) is providing a guarantee to the floor holder of a minimum investment rate of 7%, 100 basis points above the guaranteed 6% minimum level for LIBOR.. This minimum rate will be secured by means of compensation payments whenever six-month LIBOR is below 6% on the reset date for a floor (the fixing date/rollover date for the investment).

This is illustrated in the diagram opposite.

Floor: Compensating Payments

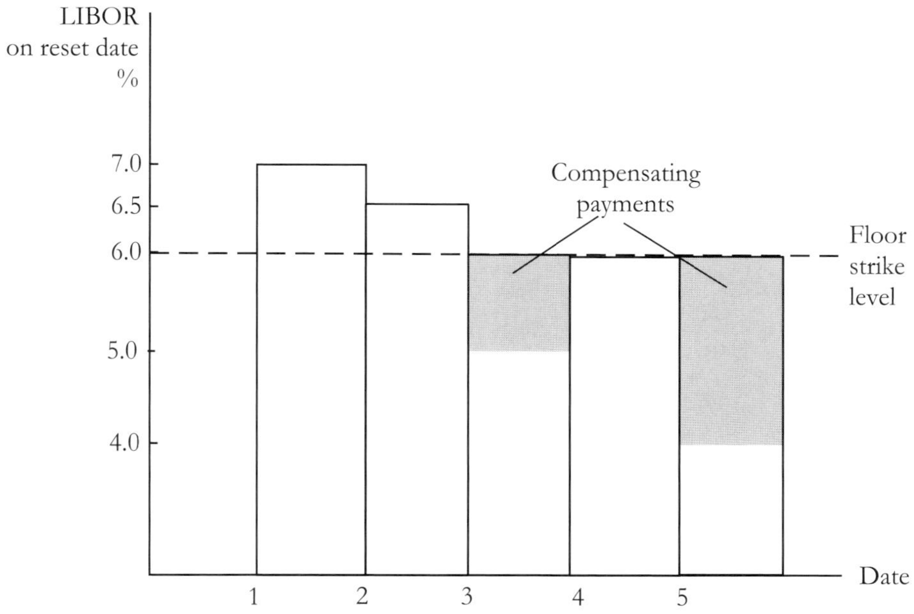

Cash flows under the floor agreement are as follows:

Premium		£(562,500)
Reset date 3	Option is exercised	
	Compensating payment =	
	$\frac{(6 - 5) \times 182 \text{ days (say)} \times £25 \text{ million}}{365 \times 100}$	£124,658
	This payment will be made at the end of the interest-rate period, on reset date 4.	
Reset date 5	Option is exercised.	
	Compensating payment, payable at the end of the interest rate period =	

$$\frac{(6 - 4) \times 182 \text{ days (for example)} \times £25 \text{ million}}{365 \times 100} = £249{,}315$$

The compensating payments put a floor of 7% per annum (6% plus 100 basis points) on investment income for the periods between reset dates 3 and 4 and for the final interest period from reset date 5.

	Six months from reset date 3	**Six months from reset date 5**
Interest rate on investment (LIBOR + 1%)	6%	5%
	£	£
Interest on £25 million investment (182 days)	747,945	623,288
Compensating amount	124,658	249,315
Total income	872,603	872,603

Total income of £872,603 represents a return of 7% per annum for a six-month (182-day) period on an investment of £25 million.

Who Uses Floors?

Interest-rate floors are used by organizations with large portfolios of variable-rate investments or variable-rate loans to customers. They are useful for companies and financial institutions that have fixed-rate payment obligations. Users include insurance companies investment companies, pension funds and banks. They are not as common as interest-rate caps.

Caps and Floors: FRAs and Interest-Rate Swaps

Just as a lender's option can be described as an option on an FRA, a cap is a call option on a series of FRAs. Similarly, a floor is a put option on a series of FRAs. A series of FRAs is similar in many respects to an interest-rate coupon swap, therefore we can compare caps and floors with interest-rate swaps.

In a plain vanilla coupon swap, the two parties to the agreement undertake to exchange interest-rate payments periodically, perhaps every six or 12 months. The interest payments are calculated on the same notional amount of principal.

- One party pays a fixed rate of interest on the notional amount of principal, and receives in return interest at a floating rate.
- The counterparty pays the floating rate of interest and receives interest at the fixed rate.

The fixed rate of interest is determined when the swap agreement is made. The floating rate of interest is determined at each swap date by reference to an agreed benchmark such as six-month or 12-month LIBOR.

In the case of plain vanilla swaps, both parties make an interest payment in each interest period. In practise, there will be just one net payment by the party owing the higher amount of interest. Because there is a payer of fixed interest and a payer of variable-rate interest in each interest period, a swap is similar to a series of consecutive FRAs.

It can be helpful when analyzing a cap or floor to use swap terminology, and refer to the buyer of a cap as paying the fixed and receiving the floating and to refer to the buyer of a floor as paying the floating and receiving the fixed. The pay/receive profiles are as follows:

	Interest payments on notional principal	
Caps		
Buy a cap	Pay fixed	Receive floating
Sell a cap	Receive fixed	Pay floating
Floors		
Buy a floor	Receive fixed	Pay floating
Sell a floor	Pay fixed	Receive floating

Coupon Swap

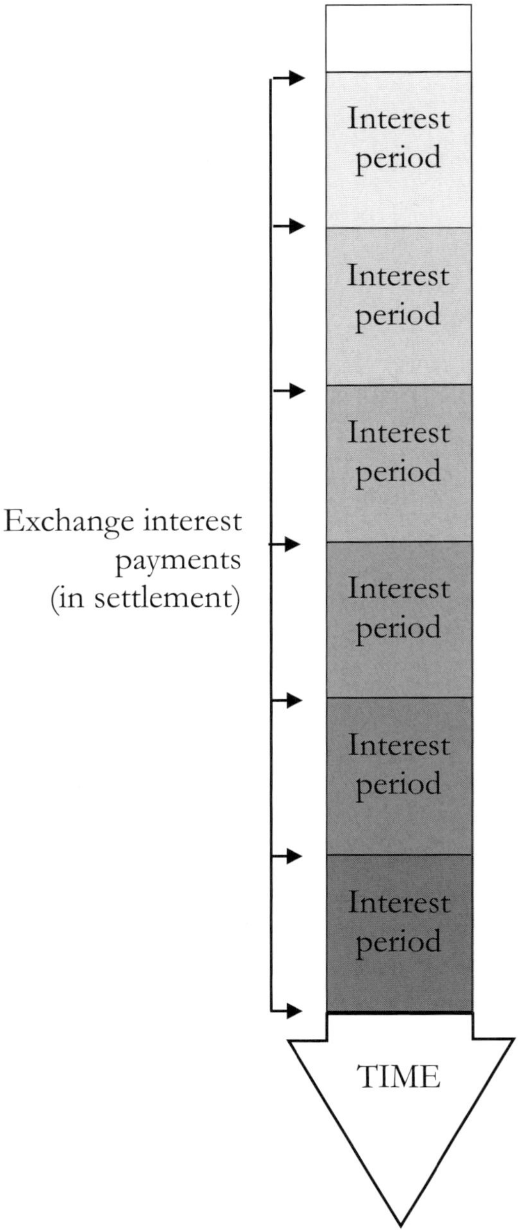

Example

A company transacts an interest-rate cap on the following terms.

Maturity	1 year
Coupon	8%
Reset frequency	Quarterly
	Note:
	First quarter = 92 days
	Second quarter = 92 days
	Third quarter = 91 days
	Fourth quarter = 90 days
Floating basis	Three-month LIBOR
Notional principal	£10 million

The three-month LIBOR rates at subsequent settlement dates are as follows:

at the end of quarter 1: 8.6%
at the end of quarter 2: 9.1%
at the end of quarter 3: 8.9%.

Analysis
The cap buyer has fixed the maximum borrowing cost by buying the cap with an 8% strike rate. Ignoring the cost of the premium for the cap, the cap-holder's cash flows can be analyzed as follows.

	End of Quarter 1 £	**End of Quarter 2** £	**End of Quarter 3** £	**End of Quarter 4** £
Pay (fixed)	-	201,644	199,452	197,260
Receive (floating	-	216,767	226,877	219,452
Net cash flow (compensation)	-	15,123	27,425	22,192

Notes
The cap does not cover the interest payment for the first quarter.

The fixed interest payment is calculated as

$$P \times \frac{8 \times D}{365 \times 100}$$

where D is the number of days in the interest period.

The variable rate receipt is calculated as

$$P \times \frac{L \times D}{365 \times 100}$$

where L is LIBOR (6% = 6, etc) and D is the number of days in the period.

The difference between paying the fixed and receiving the variable is the compensation payable to the cap holder whenever the LIBOR rate exceeds the strike rate for the cap. The compensation payment could have been calculated more simply using the formula. For example, the compensation payment for the second quarter would be

$$\frac{(8.6 - 8.0) \times 92 \text{ days} \times \pounds 10 \text{ million}}{365 \times 100}$$

$$= \pounds 15{,}123$$

Interest-Rate Collars

One disadvantage of caps or floors is the high cost of the premium. Interest-rate collars attempt to overcome this disadvantage. An interest-rate collar is a combination of a cap and a floor that can be used to obtain either

- a guaranteed maximum interest rate on floating-rate borrowings, or
- a guaranteed minimum interest rate on a floating-rate investment or a variable-rate loan.

If interest rates move in the holder's favor the benefit is limited, and in this respect collars differ from caps or floors.

- If a company wishing to maximize its interest cost chooses to buy a collar, it will not be able to benefit from any fall in the

interest rate below a floor level.
- If a company wishes to fix a minimum guaranteed yield for its investments by selling a collar, it will not be able to benefit from any rise in the interest rate above a cap level.

Collars therefore set maximum limits to potential gains as well as potential losses for the buyer and seller of the collar. For example, a company might buy an interest-rate cap, fixing the maximum rate on its variable-rate borrowing at 7% for example. The cap holder will not exercise the cap, and will benefit from a lower borrowing cost whenever the benchmark rate of interest on a reset date is below the cap level. In contrast, the same company might buy a collar instead of a cap. The collar might fix a maximum borrowing cost (cap) at 7%, but there also would be a guaranteed minimum borrowing cost. The buyer of the collar would be required to pay compensation to the seller of the collar whenever the interest rate is below a floor level on any reset date.

The benefit to the holder of a collar, over a cap or floor, is a lower premium cost. The size of the premium varies considerably according to the terms of the collar, but typically 30% less than the premium for a comparable cap or floor.

Characteristics of a Collar

A collar is in effect a combination of a cap and a floor.

To set a maximum interest rate with a collar, the buyer of the collar

- buys a cap at one strike rate and
- sells a floor at a lower strike rate.

For example, a collar might consist of buying a cap at 7% and selling a floor at 5%. This would mean that the collar buyer will pay an effective interest rate somewhere between a maximum of 7% and a minimum of 5%.

To set a minimum interest rate with a collar, the seller of the collar

- buys a floor at one stike rate and
- sells a cap at a higher strike rate.

In the example above, the seller of the cap would be fixing interest income at not less than 5%, but no more than 7%.

The premium payable for a collar is the difference between the cost of buying the cap and the premium receivable for selling the floor. Similarly, the premium receivable for selling a collar is the difference between the premium receivable from selling the cap and the premium payable for buying the floor.

Premium: Setting a Maximum Rate

Premium = Cost of buying a cap − Premium from selling a floor

Premium : Setting a Minimum Rate

Premium = Cost of buying a floor − Premium from selling a cap

Compensating payments are made at the end of each interest-rate period to which they relate, in the same way as for caps and floors.

Buying a Collar : Buying a Cap and Selling a Floor

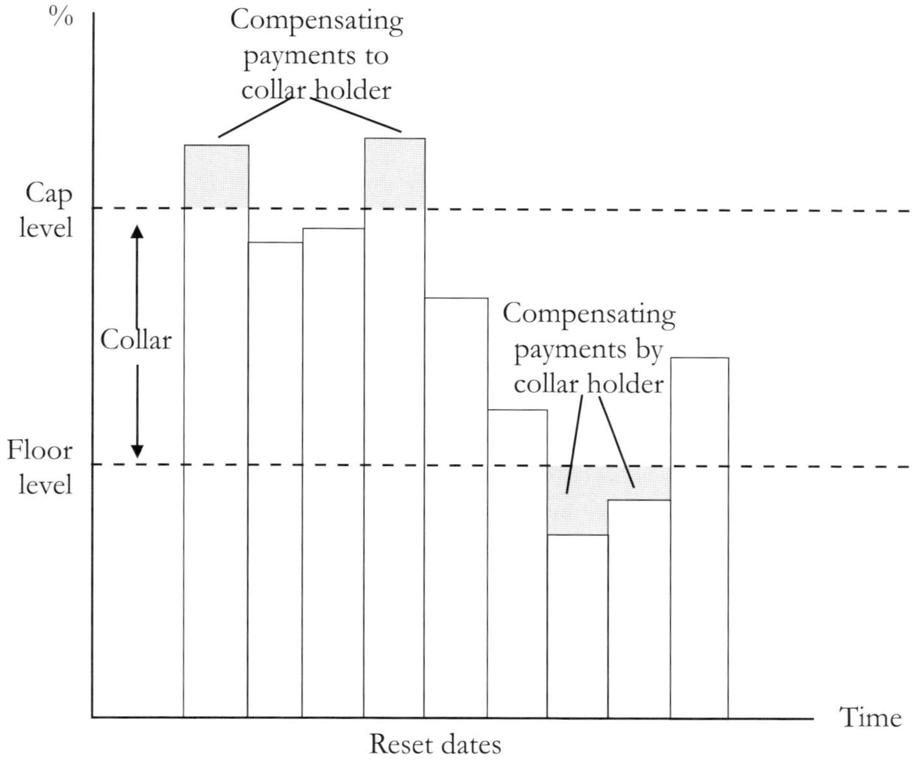

Example

A company has £20 million of floating-rate debt, with rollover dates every three months, on which it pays interest at LIBOR + 50 basis points. Three-month LIBOR is currently 7%, but the rate has been volatile and is expected to remain volatile in the future. The company wants to ensure that borrowing costs do not exceed 8.5% for the next two years. The premium cost of an interest-rate cap at a strike level of 8% is more than the company is willing to pay, and so the company arranges with its bank to transact a collar of between 5% and 8% on three-month LIBOR. The net premium agreed is 120 basis points, after subtracting the premium receivable for writing a floor at 5% from the cost of buying a cap at 8%.

The terms of the collar are

Underlying index	Three-month LIBOR
Terms of the collar	Two years
Reset dates	Every three months
Notional principal amount	£20 million
Cap strike level	8%
Floor strike level	5%
Payment terms	Quarterly in arrears
Premium (net premium paid for cap and received for floor)	120 basis points (£240,000)

Analysis
The company has, in effect, bought a cap at 8%, guaranteeing a maximum borrowing cost of 8.5% (8% + 50 basis points). At the same time it has sold a floor, giving a minimum borrowing cost of 5.5% (5% + 50 basis points).

Suppose that three-month LIBOR on the first four reset dates is 6%, 4.5%, 7.5% and 9% respectively. Compensation payments will become payable as follows:

Reset date	Three-month LIBOR	Outcome
1	6%	Neither option will be exercised and no compensation payments become payable by either party because LIBOR is between 5% and 8% inclusive. LIBOR must be above 8% for the collar holder's cap option to be exercised and below 5% for the collar writer's floor option to be exercised.
2	4.5%	Because LIBOR is below 5%, the bank selling the collar will exercise its option to fix the minimum rate at 5%. The collar buyer will become

Reset date	Three-month LIBOR	Outcome (continued)
		liable for a compensation payment to the bank (collar writer).
3	7.5%	Neither option will be exercised and no compensation payments become payable by either party because LIBOR is between 5% and 8% inclusive.
4	9%	Because LIBOR is above 8%, the collar holder will exercise the option to limit the cost of borrowing. A compensation payment will become payable by the bank (collar writer) to the collar holder.

Assuming in each case a quarter of 91 days, the following compensation payments will be payable.

At reset date 2, the collar holder will become liable to pay the collar seller (bank) a compensation payment. This is payable quarterly in arrears on reset date 3. The amount is calculated as follows:

$$\frac{(5 - 4.5) \times 91 \times £20 \text{ million}}{365 \times 100}$$

$$= £24{,}932$$

This will be added to the interest payable on the £20 million loan that is 5% (LIBOR of 4.5% plus 50 basis points) for the period. The compensation payment will bring the total payments on the loan to an effective rate of 5.5% (minimum guaranteed LIBOR rate of 5% plus 0.5%).

At reset date 4, the bank will become liable to the collar holder for a compensation payment. This is payable quarterly in arrears on reset date 5. The amount is calculated as follows:

$$\frac{(9-8) \times 91 \times £20 \text{ million}}{365 \times 100}$$

$$= £49{,}863$$

The effective cost of borrowing for the company will be as follows:

From	To	Interest on loan at LIBOR + 0.5%	Compensation payment	Total cost
		%	%	%
Start of collar agreement	Reset date 1	7.5	-	7.5
Reset date 1	Reset date 2	6.5	-	6.5
Reset date 2	Reset date 3	5.0	+ 0.5	5.5
Reset date 3	Reset date 4	8.0	-	8.0
Reset date 4	Reset date 5	9.5	–1.0	8.5

Because the company that buys a collar from its bank might have to make compensating payments, the bank will be accepting some *credit risk* when it sells a collar. The company's lines of credit with the bank will be affected accordingly.

Zero-Cost Collars

If a company is particularly anxious to avoid paying any premium at all, it may be able to negotiate a zero-cost collar. Under this arrangement, the premium paid for buying the cap equals the premium received for selling the floor, leaving no premium to pay. The strike levels for the cap and the floor would have to be set accordingly. The collar will have a similar effect to a swap from floating-rate debt into a fixed-rate debt (or a floating-rate investment into a fixed-rate investment) because the cap and floor-strike levels would be very close to each other. For example, if the cap has a strike level of 7.25% and the floor has a strike level of

7.125%, the effective interest rate for the collar holder would be restricted to a 7.125% - 7.25% range, almost a fixed rate.

Example

A zero-cost collar is arranged whereby the collar holder buys a cap on three-month sterling at 8% over a two-year period, and sells a floor on three-month sterling at 7.5%.

	Strike rate	**Premium**
Three-month sterling cap	8.0%	75 basis points
Three-month sterling floor	7.5%	75 basis points

The net cost of the premium is zero and the collar holder's effective borrowing cost may fluctuate between 8% and 7.5%. This is a narrow band that almost fixes the effective borrowing for the two years.

Summary

Caps, floors and collars are derivatives of interest-rate options. They provide *medium-term* interest-rate guarantees and at the same time allow the holder of the cap, floor or, to a lesser extent collar, to benefit from favorable market interest rates.

They are used by companies to hedge interest-rate exposures for large amounts of principal. However, the cost of premiums can be high, particularly for caps and floors. Collars are cheaper, but with a zero-cost collar, the interest-rate spread would be very narrow, severely limiting the holder's ability to benefit from favorable interest-rate movements.

5

Option Prices

For over-the-counter options, the strike price or strike rate is chosen by the customer buying the option. Option buyers can stipulate whatever strike price they wish, but the option writer will charge a higher or lower premium accordingly. With options on interest-rate futures, the available strike prices are decided by the futures and options exchange, but several strike prices will be available for any given expiry date. The market price of options for the same expiry date will differ according to their strike price.

Indicative Prices

Banks that are active in OTC options trading, and seek to encourage options customers, might supply indicative prices for OTC option premiums on a screen-based information system such as Reuters, but it is more usual for prices to be quoted over the phone in response to customers' requests.

Prices quoted on screen are indicative only, and based on the assumptions of:

- an at-the-money strike price
- a small-sized deal, and
- a reasonably large corporate customer of the size likely to use screen-based price-information systems.

For larger deals, the customer should be able to negotiate a smaller premium.

The majority of interest-rate options are out-of-the-money when written, and the premium will be less than the at-the-money option rates displayed on a price-information screen. Most options are out-of-the-money when written because they are used to limit the impact of adverse interest-rate movements. Because it is cheaper to buy an option at a less favorable strike price, some adverse movement is tolerated.

Pricing Models

Banks use mathematical models to calculate the premium for the options they write. Pricing models, such as the Black-Scholes model, are based on a theory of options pricing that is outlined in this chapter. When a customer calls to discuss terms for buying an option, the bank will feed the option details into the model that will then calculate a premium.

- An OTC option is priced when it is written, and its original value is the premium paid by the buyer. However, the value of an option will change over time. Banks and other organizations that deal in options will monitor their options continually, and re-value them to their current value, a process known as marking-to-market. Any change in the value of an option is recorded as a profit or loss for the options trading desk, depending on whether the option has risen or fallen in value, and whether the option has been bought or sold.
- Exchange-traded options have a visible market price. Gains or losses on positions in these options can be measured by the change in market price over time.

Pricing Theory

The basic theory of options pricing is the same for all options; interest-rate options, currency options, stock options, etc.

The cost of a premium depends on several factors:

- the interest rate (strike price) specified in the option, and whether this is at-the-money, in-the-money or out-of-the-money
- the length of time to the expiry date
- the expected volatility of the interest rate in the time up to the expiry of the option
- whether the option can be exercised at any time up to expiry (American-style) or on the expiry date only (European-style). American-style options may have a higher premium than similar European-style options
- the length of the interest-rate period to which the option relates. The length of this period affects the amount of compensation payable if the option is exercised. This has an influence on the price charged for the option
- the interest rate receivable on cash deposits between the time the option is written and the expiry date. The writer of an option can invest the money received for the premium, and the interest earned in the period up to exercise/expiry should reduce the premium charged to the option buyer.

Interest Value and Time Value

Option pricing theory identifies two components to the premium: an intrinsic value and a time value. The premium is the sum of these two values.

OPTION PREMIUM
is the sum of

INTRINSIC VALUE	TIME VALUE
Influences:	Influences:
Strike price	Time to expiry
Current market price	Volatility of market interest rates
	Length of interest-rate period
	Interest rate in period to expiry

Intrinsic value can be negative, but because an option writer would not write an option for a negative total premium, the value of a premium must exceed zero for the option to be written and sold.

Intrinsic Value

The intrinsic value of an interest-rate option is the difference between its strike price and the current benchmark rate of interest, applied to the notional principal of the option. The strike price might be the same as the current benchmark rate, more favorable to the option buyer than the benchmark rate, or less favorable to the option buyer. Intrinsic value therefore might be zero, a positive amount or a negative value.

Strike price compared with current market rate of interest	Name given to the option	Intrinsic value
Same	At-the-money	Nil
More favorable	In-the-money	Positive - the value of the difference between the strike price and the current benchmark rate.
Less favorable	Out-of-the-money	Negative - the value of the difference between the strike price and the current benchmark rate.

Because an option will be exercised only if it is in-the-money, it must have a positive intrinsic value when it is exercised. If it has a zero or negative intrinsic value it will be allowed to lapse on expiry date.

Note

A European-style option is at-the-money when its strike price equals the

FRA rate (the forward/forward rate) for the interest period to which the option relates. As an option approaches expiry, the forward/forward rate will move closer to the current spot market rate, and at expiry it will be the same as the current spot rate.

Example 1
The strike price for a European-style borrower's option on one-year LIBOR is 6% for a notional loan period starting in three months' time. The current forward/forward rate for one-year LIBOR in three months' time, i.e. the 3 v 15 forward rate, is 7.5%. The option therefore is in-the-money by 1.5% per annum, and the intrinsic value of the option is 1.5% of the notional principal.

If the market rate for one-year LIBOR had been 5% instead of 7.5%, the option would have had a negative intrinsic value of 1% (6% - 5%) of the notional principal.

Example 2
The strike price for a European-style lender's option is 8% for six-month LIBOR on a notional loan starting in four months' time, and the current 4 v 10 forward rate for six-month LIBOR is 6%. The option is in-the-money by 2%. Because it is an option for a six-month deposit, the intrinsic value is 1% (2% x 6/12) of the notional principal.

Time Value

Time value is a value placed on an option to reflect the possibility that market rates will move in the period up to the expiry of the option, to the benefit of the option holder. When there is a greater possibility that rates could move in the option-holder's favor, time value will be higher and the option will cost more. If an interest-rate option is out-of-the-money when written, the likelihood that it eventually will be exercised depends on:

- by how much the benchmark rate of interest will have to

change before the option becomes in-the-money (the option's intrinsic value becomes positive), and
- the probability that the benchmark rate of interest might change in the option holder's favor in the time to expiry.

An interest-rate option could be in-the-money when written. In the period to expiry, market rates might change so as to make the option even more deeply in-the-money that would increase the option holder's gain and the option writer's loss. Thus in-the-money options also have a time value.

Interest-rate options provide three main elements in time value:

- time to expiry
- volatility of interest rates
- the market interest rate (benchmark rate).

Time to Expiry

For an interest-rate option with a longer time to expiry, there is a greater probability of the market rate moving against the option writer and in favor of the option holder. Suppose for example that we compare two options identical in every respect except for their expiry date.

	Option A	**Option B**
Type	Borrower's	Borrower's
Strike price	7% (3-month LIBOR)	7% (3-month LIBOR)
Notional principal	$10 million	$10 million
Style	European-style	European-style
Expiry date	June 30	August 31

If both options are written on the same date, Option B will be more expensive because its expiry date is two months later than for Option A. In those two months, there must be some chance that three-month LIBOR will move further against the option writer. Consequently, the option holder should be expected to pay more for the option.

Time Decay

The time value of an option should fall as it approaches expiry. This fall in value over time is known as time decay that can be estimated mathematically using option-pricing models. Time decay becomes more rapid as the option gets closer to its expiry date because the likelihood of a large further interest-rate movement in the remaining time to expiry diminishes substantially.

Time Decay Curve

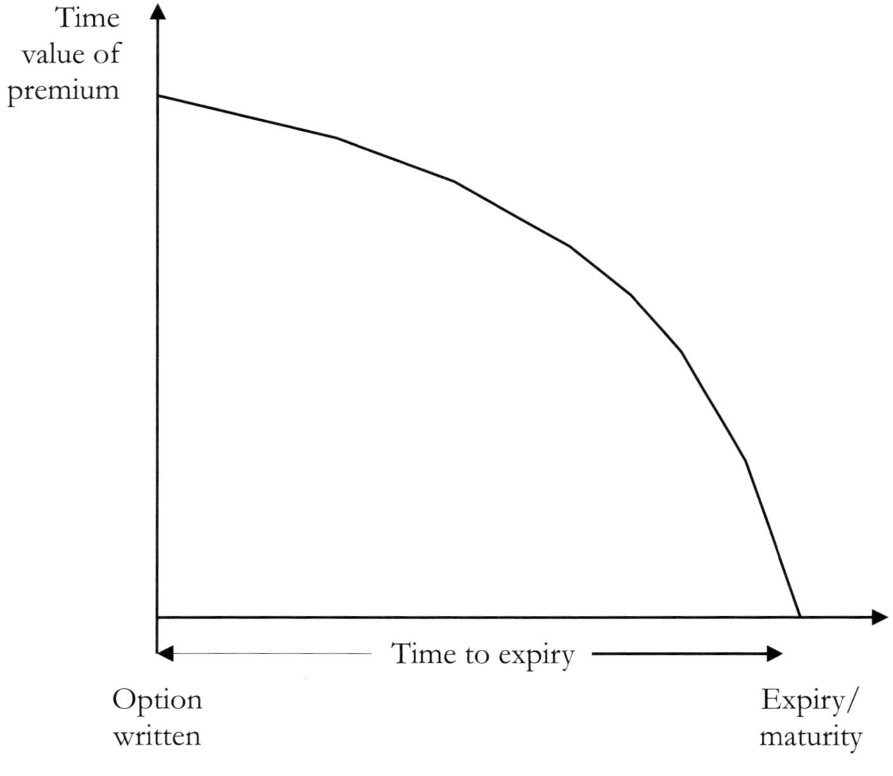

Volatility of Interest Rates
The reason for buying interest-rate options is uncertainty about future interest-rate movements. When rate movements could be large, and in either direction, options will have a greater value than when interest-rate movements are expected to be fairly small, or in a predictable direction. Greater interest-rate volatility therefore adds to the value/cost of an option.

Volatility is a measure of the movements in the market price for a financial instrument, both in terms of size of price changes and direction or directions of change (up or down). Suppose for example that six-month LIBOR is more volatile than three-month LIBOR. If this were the case, an option on six-month LIBOR would cost more than an option on three-month LIBOR written at the same time and for the same expiry date.

The volatility of an interest rate can change over time. The cost or value of an option will change as volatility in the price of the underlying item changes. If, for example, the volatility of three-month LIBOR increases between Year 1 and Year 2, a bank writing an option on three-month LIBOR in Year 2 will charge more than in Year 1 for an identical option.

Volatility must be measured for option-pricing models, and there are two broad measures, historical volatility and implied volatility.

Historical Volatility

The historical variations in the interest rate can be measured for a selected period in the past. For the purpose of mathematical modelling, volatility would be measured statistically as a standard deviation of variations around an average rate of variation in the period during which the measurements were taken. The measurement of historical volatility is explained in the appendix to this book.

Implied Volatility

When the price of an interest-rate option is known, interest-rate volatility can be implied from the price by using an option pricing model in reverse. By feeding the premium and all other variables into the model, the measurement of volatility comes out as the balancing figure. This implied volatility could then be used for pricing new options to customers.

Measuring implied volatility from market prices for exchange-traded interest-rate options is also possible to put a measurement to the market's perception of volatility. Implied volatility can be compared with historical volatility, as a method of estimating what future volatility might be.

- If options traders expect an option to trade at a higher volatility in the future, they will buy volatility, i.e. buy the option.
- If options traders expect an option to trade at a lower volatility in the future, they will sell volatility, i.e. sell the options.

Although option-pricing models need a mathematical measurement of volatility, there are probably still many options traders who believe that in practise, the assessment of volatility calls for judgment by the trader rather than measurement by mathematical modeling.

Market Interest Rates

The cost of an option also depends to some extent on the current rates of interest in the market. The option premium normally is payable when the option is written, but the option holder can exercise his rights only at some time in the future. The premium therefore should be discounted to take account of the benefit to the option writer of its up-front payment from the buyer. If market rates of interest go up, option premiums should fall.

Example

A European-style lender's option on three-month LIBOR with an expiry date in six months would cost £5,000 if the premium were payable on the expiry date. The premium however is payable now and should be discounted.

- If the six-month rate of interest (the time to expiry date) is 10% per annum, the premium would be discounted by 5% (6/12 x 10%) and the amount of the premium should be £4,762 (£5,000 ÷ 1.05).
- If the six-month rate of interest is higher, at 14% per annum, the premium would be discounted by 7% to £4,673 (£5,000 ÷ 1.07) and therefore would be lower.

Deltas, Gammas, Thetas and Vegas

Dealers in options use a number of ratios for monitoring changes in options prices in response to changes in factors that affect their intrinsic value or time value.

Delta Values

Delta is a ratio that measures the change in an option's price or value in relation to a change in the market price of the underlying item or instrument to which the option relates. For interest-rate options, this is the benchmark interest rate.

$$\text{Delta} = \frac{\text{Change in option premium/value}}{\text{Change in benchmark interest rate}}$$

The value of an option's delta could be anything between zero and one, and it is not constant at every interest-rate level. An option's delta will change as the interest rate changes.

- An option that is deeply in-the-money and with a short time to expiry will have little or no time value, and its price will consist almost entirely of intrinsic value. A change in the market rate/ price of the underlying item will alter the intrinsic value of the option by the same amount, or nearly the same amount, and the delta of the option therefore will be 1.0, or nearly 1.0.
- An option that is deeply out-of-the-money has a negative intrinsic value, and a change in the spot price is unlikely to affect the value of the option by much, if at all. The delta of the option will be 0 or close to 0.
- An option that is at-the-money has a delta of about 0.5.

Delta Values

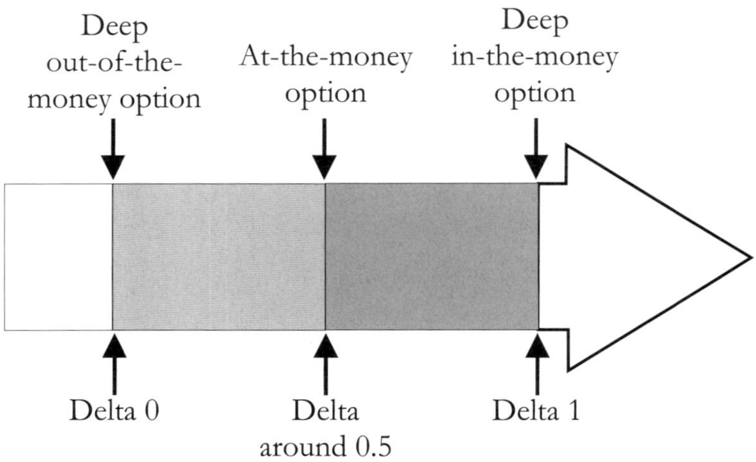

Delta values are useful for a number of reasons.

- Delta is a useful ready measure for estimating the likely change in the option's premium/value should an interest-rate change occur.
- Options traders might use a hedging technique known as delta hedging. Banks that deal in options can hedge their options positions by purchasing or selling FRAs or interest-rate swaps. Delta hedging provides a method of deciding how much to buy or sell.

Delta Hedging

Delta hedging is a system of trading rules that uses a mathematical options-pricing model to calculate the approximate size of hedge that a writer of options should obtain to minimize the risks from his trading position. It is used primarily by banks to calculate the size of the hedge they need for their options-trading positions. The delta value of an option can be used to quantify the amount of principal for a FRA or swap that should be bought or sold to create a suitable hedge.

For example, suppose that a bank writes a borrower's option with an at-the-money strike rate on notional principal of $20 million. If the delta for the option is 0.50, the bank can hedge its options position by buying an FRA on \$10 million (0.50 x \$20 million) for the same forward interest period to which the option relates.

If it becomes more likely as time passes that the option will be exercised, its delta value will rise. If the likelihood of the option being exercised diminishes, its delta will fall.

Continuing with the example, suppose that interest rates rise, and the probability that the option will be exercised therefore increases. The delta of the borrower's option also will rise. If it rises from 0.50 to 0.60, the bank should increase the size of its hedge to \$12 million (0.60 x \$20 million), to regain delta neutrality. It can do this by buying an FRA on \$2 million, to add to its FRA on \$10 million for the same interest period.

If the delta of the option fell because the likelihood of the option being exercised diminishes, the hedge would be reduced in size by selling an FRA.

The delta for an at-the-money option should be about 0.50. As an option approaches expiry, its delta should move towards 1.0 if it is in-the-money and towards 0 if it is deeply out-of-the-money.

The diagram overleaf summarizes the concept. The delta curve shows the delta value of a call option at different interest rates, rising from zero to one, and the percentage of the option's notional principal that should be hedged by purchasing or selling FRAs or swaps.

Delta Hedging

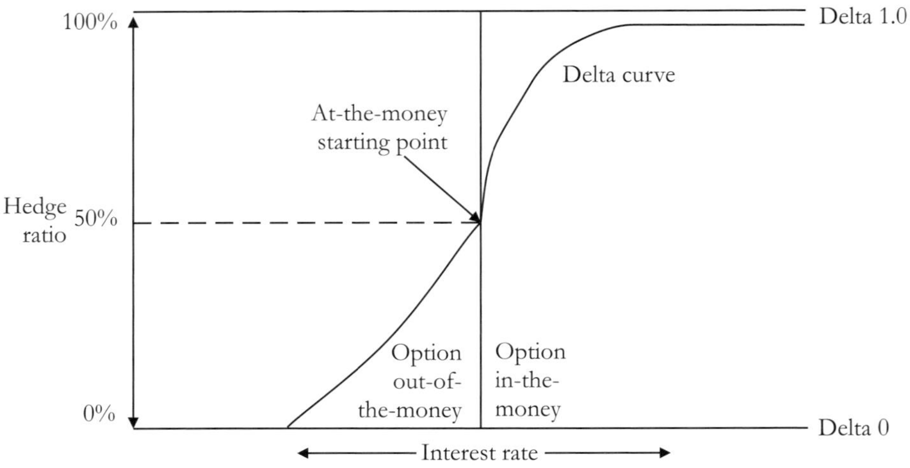

An application of delta hedging for an interest-rate option position is illustrated in the appendix to this book.

Gammas, Thetas and Vegas

Other options ratios used by dealers are gammas, thetas and vegas.

Gamma

A gamma ratio for an interest-rate option is the ratio of the underlying rate of change in the option's delta to the rate of change in the underlying interest rate. A trader tracks the gamma of an option because it shows by how much he has to change his delta hedge whenever the price of the underlying item changes. The gamma for an option is not a constant value but changes with movements in the underlying item (interest rate) and as the remaining time to expiry diminishes.

Theta

A theta value measures the amount by which an option's value declines as time elapses. It is measured as follows:

$$\text{Theta} = \frac{\%\ \text{change in option premium/value}}{\%\ \text{change in time to expiry}}$$

Because the option price falls as the option approaches expiry due to time decay, an option's theta is a higher value close to expiry, and lower when there is a longer time remaining to expiry. Theta therefore is used as a measure of the time decay of an option.

Vega

A vega ratio measures the change in an option's premium relative to the change in the price volatility of the underlying item (the interest rate).

$$\text{Vega} = \frac{\text{Change in value of option}}{\text{Change in volatility}}$$

Vega always must be a positive value. If volatility increases, the value of an option, call or put, also will rise. The vega ratio can be useful for monitoring the significance of interest-rate volatility for option premiums.

Summary

An option premium is the sum of its intrinsic value and its time value.

- When an option is out-of-the-money, there is less prospect of the option being exercised or having a high value to the buyer because it would need a movement in the price of the underlying item (the benchmark interest rate) to bring it in-the-money. An out-of-the-money option has a negative intrinsic value. Its time value will depend on how far out-of-the-money the option is, and on other factors such as the remaining time to expiry of the option and the volatility in the price of the underlying item.
- The further an option is in-the-money, the more its intrinsic value will determine its price. When the price of the underlying

item changes, the price of an in-the-money option will change by the same, or nearly the same, amount.

Volatility in the underlying interest rate is a significant influence on time value. A mathematical measurement of volatility can be extracted from historical price data.

The appendix to this book explains how historical volatility is measured and describes an option-pricing model and a delta hedge.

Using OTC Options

An organization not specializing in options trading should identify a need or an opportunity before it decides to purchase an interest-rate option. The treasury department of a non-bank organization might also decide to write interest-rate options, but there is a risk of high losses in the event of an unfavorable and large movement in the interest rate. Non-bank organizations should control the writing of options by their finance staff in treasury.

Elements in the decision to buy an option (open a position) are:

- a large variable-rate loan or deposit that the organization either has or expects to have in the foreseeable future
- concern about the volatility of interest rates over the next few months
- the effect on borrowing costs or income from deposits of an adverse change in interest rates.

Example
A construction company is financing a development with a variable-rate loan of £20 million. Interest is payable at LIBOR + 1.5%, and the rollover dates are annual. The next rollover date is in three months on 1 July, and work on the development is expected to be finished in fifteen months. Currently 12-month LIBOR is 5.5%. A general election is imminent and the company is concerned about the effect a change of government could have on interest rates. It does not want interest costs for the final 12-month period of the development to exceed 10% per annum.

Analysis

Here the company has identified an interest-rate problem that needs to be resolved. It could discuss arrangements for a borrower's option with its bank. The bank could offer to write a European-style option on £20 million at a strike price of 7% on 12-month LIBOR, for a premium of 150 basis points (1.5% of the notional principal). This would secure 10% as the worst-case, all-in-cost for the company.

	%
Premium (per annum)	1.5
Worst-case rate locked in by option	7.0
Margin above LIBOR on loan	1.5
Full cost	10.0

If the company's fears about interest rates do not materialize, borrowing costs will be less than 10% per annum, after allowing for the 1.5% premium that the company has paid as a hedge against the interest-rate risk.

Approaching a Bank

Negotiations between an organization wishing to purchase an option and its bank (the option writer) normally will be conducted by phone. The premium will be agreed as part of these discussions. The deal will be confirmed by the bank, usually within 24 hours. The confirmation will set out the details of the option agreement.

An out-of-the-money option is bought more frequently. The option therefore would be exercised only if market interest rates move adversely and by a fairly large margin for the borrower or lender in the period up to expiry date. The advantage of an out-of-the-money option, however, is its lower premium cost.

In the UK, an option buyer will pay the bank (option writer):

- for same-day value, for interest-rate options on sterling, or

- in two business days for interest-rate options on all other currencies, reflecting the normal two-day settlement period for spot currency transactions.

Example 1

Alpha, a UK company, is about to launch a takeover bid for a target company, Beta, with the aim that it will liquidate Beta's business and sell off its assets within a few months of acquiring control.

The finance director of Alpha negotiates a term loan for £400 million from a small consortium of banks, at an interest rate of LIBOR plus 50 basis points. The loan is for one year. The terms of the loan give Alpha the right to repay the loan in full at any reset date. Reset dates will be every three months. If Alpha does not repay the loan until the end of the 12-month term, the loan will be rolled over at each reset date.

Sterling interest rates are beginning to rise at the short end of the yield curve, and Alpha estimates that interest costs could have a noticeable effect on the profitability of the takeover deal, should three-month interest rates rise much further.

The directors of Alpha have discussed the cost of the loan finance. They will need to borrow the funds in one month's time. They agree that the following course of action might be appropriate.

Action

Alpha should buy a series of borrowers' options (a cap). The options would be on notional principal of £400 million. Each option would be for a three-month interest period to coincide with the reset dates on the loan. The borrower's options required will be:

- a call option on a 1 v 4 FRA, i.e. on a three-month notional loan of £400 million starting in one month's time
- a call option on a 4 v 7 FRA, i.e. on a three-month notional loan of £400 million starting in four months' time
- a call option on a 7 v 10 FRA, i.e. on a three-month notional loan of £400 million starting in seven months' time

- a call option on a 10 v 13 FRA, i.e. on a three-month notional loan of £400 million starting in ten months' time.

Example 2

Zincbetter is a large trading company. Its cash flows are seasonal and it experiences two periods of cash surplus each year and two periods during which it needs to borrow to finance a cash deficit. The finance director of the company is annoyed that interest rates seem to be high whenever the company is in debt, but seem to be low whenever the company has a cash surplus. He discusses the problem with his bank, commenting that he would like to ensure that interest costs over the next three years will never exceed 8% per annum and cash investment yields will never be less than 4%.

The cash flow forecasts for the company for the next three-year period indicate that for each of the three years, there will be a core borrowing requirement or a core cash surplus for investing, as follows:

1 January-31 March	Surplus cash	$20 million
1 April-30 June	Core borrowing requirement	$60 million
1 July-30 September	Surplus cash	$30 million
1 October-31 December	Core borrowing requirement	$40 million

Analysis

One method of trying to ensure that interest costs do not rise above 8% would be to buy a series of seasonal borrowers' options, covering the periods when there will be borrowing requirements.

Caps

Year	Period each year	Notional principal	Interest period
1, 2 and 3	1 April-30 June	$60 million	Three months
1, 2 and 3	1 October-31 December	$40 million	Three months

To try to ensure that yields on cash invested do not fall below 4%, the company could buy a series of seasonal lenders' options.

Floors

Year	Period each year	Notional principal	Interest period
1, 2 and 3	1 January-31 March	$20 million	Three months
1, 2 and 3	1 July-30 September	$30 million	Three months

The disadvantage of caps and floors is their cost. An alternative would be to arrange several seasonal collars, possibly at a zero cost or as close to a zero cost as possible. Each collar would be for a three-month interest period, as follows:

Period each year	Collar arrangement	Notional principal
1 January-31 March	Buy floor, sell cap	$20 million
1 April-30 June	Buy cap, sell floor	$60 million
1 July-30 September	Buy floor, sell cap	$30 million
1 October-31 December	Buy cap, sell floor	$40 million

Closing a Position

An option holder automatically closes a position when the option is exercised or expires. Occasionally, however, the holder might decide before expiry that the option is no longer required. Plans for future borrowings could be canceled for example, ending the requirement for a borrower's option. Similarly, expectations of future cash holdings to place on deposit might not occur, ending the requirement for a lender's option.

The option holder cannot sell the option to someone else because borrowers' and lenders' options are OTC options that are specific agreements with an individual bank. Unlike exchange-traded options, OTC options do not have a second-hand market for buying and selling. There are, however, three possible courses of action:

- Continue to hold the option as a speculative investment and hope the option will be profitable to exercise on expiry. The maximum loss would be the cost of the premium already paid, and this will occur if the option is allowed to lapse on expiry.

- Ask the bank to cancel the option agreement, and negotiate a part-repayment of the premium based on market interest-rate levels at the time of the cancelation. The bank would not be willing to do this unless it considers that the option still has some value.
- Write an option that reverses the original transaction and receive any realization value in the form of a premium. For example, suppose a company has purchased a six-month European option to receive fixed interest for one year at 11%. After three months the option is no longer required. The company can sell a three-month option to pay fixed interest for one year at 11% and achieve a perfectly matched position. The option premium will reflect the time value of the remaining three months plus any intrinsic value that the option may hold at prevailing interest rates. The ability to write options is limited to organizations that can find customers to buy them. Therefore only a bank or a very large company whose treasury department has a quasi-banking capability and is acceptable to banks who would be the option buyers, could write options.

Who Uses Options?

Option buyers are

- banks
- financial institutions
- government agencies/local authorities
- investment companies
- large non-financial companies
- occasionally, wealthy private individuals.

Most banks are prepared to write OTC options for their large customers. The size of the OTC market is difficult to judge, but the volume of deals will be higher when there is greater market uncertainty about the future course of short-term interest rates.

The size of the exchange-traded market is much more visible because trading volumes and the number of open positions are reported. An open position in an option exists when an option has been bought/sold, and the position has not yet been closed by expiry or exercise of the option, or by means of an offsetting sale or purchase of matching options.

7

Options on Interest-Rate Futures

Borrowers' and lenders' options, and caps, floors and collars are all over-the-counter options, negotiated individually with a bank. The only exchange-traded interest-rate options are options on interest-rate futures. These are bought and sold on futures exchanges such as the London International Financial Futures Market (LIFFE), Eurex, the International Monetary Market (IMM) of the Chicago Mercantile Exchange (CME), the Chicago Board of Trade (CBOT), Matif and MEFF.

Interest-Rate Futures

Some understanding of futures is needed to appreciate options on futures. Briefly, an interest-rate future is a standardized forward contract for the purchase on a specified future date of a quantity of bonds (long-term interest-rate futures) or a notional short-term deposit of funds (short-term interest-rate futures) at a rate of interest that is agreed in the buying price for the future.

For example, a three-month euribor future traded on LIFFE is a contract for a three-month deposit of €1,000,000, at an interest rate (a euribor rate) agreed when the future is bought and sold. The buyer of a euribor future is agreeing to receive a deposit of €1,000,000 for three months at the agreed rate of interest, from the settlement date of the future. It might be helpful to think of a buyer as someone who is contracting to receive the agreed rate of interest on the euros deposit. A buyer might be a bank or investment company wishing to secure an interest rate for anticipated lending or investing. The seller of a euribor future is agreeing to provide a €1,000,000 deposit for three months at the agreed rate of interest. It might help to think of a seller as someone who is contracting to pay the agreed rate of interest on the euros deposit. A company might sell a future if it wishes to secure an interest rate for anticipated borrowing.

Widely traded futures contracts for which there are also options on the futures include the following:

Interest-Rate Futures for which Options are Traded

Contract	Exchange trading	Unit of
Short-term interest-rate futures		
Three month sterling deposit (sterling LIBOR)	LIFFE	£500,000
Three-month euros deposit (euribor)	LIFFE	€1,000,000
Three-month eurodollar deposit	CME	$1,000,000
Three-month euroswiss deposit	LIFFE	SFr 1,000,000
13-week US Treasury bills	CME	$1,000,000
Bond futures		
Notional 7% UK govt bonds (long gilt)	LIFFE	£100,000
Notional 30-year 6% US Treasury bonds	CBOT	$100,000
Notional 8.5-10.5 year 7% German government bonds	Eurex	€100,000
Notional 8.5-10.5 year 3.5% German or French government bonds	Matif	€100,000
Notional 30-year 6.5% Spanish government bonds	MEFF	€100,000

Interest-rate futures are traded by banks, other financial institutions and large companies that wish to hedge interest-rate risk or possibly to speculate for profit on movements in interest rates and futures prices. For an organization wanting to hedge an interest-rate risk

- selling futures can lock in an effective interest rate for borrowing
- buying futures can lock in an effective interest rate for lending or investing.

Settlement dates for futures contracts are standard dates set by the exchange. Futures are traded for settlement at quarterly intervals, typically in March, June, September and December. Depending on the exchange and the contract, futures contracts are traded at any time for a number of the next delivery months, for example for the next eight or ten delivery months.

For long-term interest-rate futures, bonds are physically delivered when the future reaches its settlement date in exchange for their agreed purchase price. A futures contract is for notional government bonds, but each exchange has rules for the delivery of equivalent actual bonds. Most futures contracts do not reach their delivery date, however, because buyers or sellers of futures usually unwind their trading position before the expiry date for the future.

Short-term interest futures provide for a final cash settlement for difference at settlement date, and physical delivery of the underlying short-term funds does not take place. Again, relatively few short-term interest-rate futures, known as STIR futures, reach settlement because buyers or sellers of the contracts unwind their trading positions before then.

A position is unwound and closed simply by making an offsetting trade in the futures for the same delivery date. For example, a buyer of 100 March euribor futures can close his/her position before the contract expires in March by selling 100 March euribor futures. There will be an overall profit or loss on the futures trading, depending on the diference between the buying price and the selling price for the 100 contracts.

Pricing Futures

The method of pricing futures differs between short-term and long-term interest-rate futures.

- Short-term interest-rate futures are priced as an index value down from 100, and the price is set by subtracting the interest rate from 100. For example, if a future on a short-term sterling deposit is sold at an interest rate of 6%, the sale price for the future would be 94.00. Similarly, if a future on a short-term eurodollar deposit is sold at an interest rate of 5.5%, the sale price for the future would be 94.50. The value of each movement in price of 0.01 (one basis point or one hundredth of one per cent) has a standard value. For a three-month eurodollar future, this is $25 that represents interest at 0.01% per annum for three months on a deposit of $1,000,000. For a three-month sterling (short sterling) future the value of a price movement of 0.01 is £12.50, representing interest for three months at 0.01% on a deposit of £500,000.

- Long-term (bond) futures are traded at a price per £100, $100 or €100 etc. nominal value of the bonds. For example, a price of 96 for a long gilt future would be £96 per £100 nominal value of the underlying notional gilt. A price movement of 0.01 (one tick) has a standard value, £10 on £100,000 of government bonds (0.01% of £100,000).

Futures contracts are traded between buyer and seller at an agreed contract price. After the contract is made and in the period up to settlement, the market price for the future might go up or down. For example, if interest rates on three-month sterling fell from 6% to 5.75%, the price of a short-sterling future would rise from 94.00 to 94.25. Similarly, if interest rates went up from 6.5% to 7.9%, the price would fall from 93.50 to 92.10.

An increase in the market price of a future represents a profit for anyone who has already bought and a loss for anyone who has already sold. For example, suppose that Alpha sells a three-month June sterling future to Beta at a price of 93.00. If the price subsequently changes to 93.75, Beta will make a gain of 0.75 (or 75 ticks) and Alpha will make a corresponding loss. Beta has bought a sterling deposit at an interest rate of 7%, and because market rates have now fallen to 6.25%, Beta has gained. By selling futures at 93.00 Alpha has undertaken to pay 7% from June on a notional three-month sterling deposit of £500,000, and therefore has lost out from the fall in the market rate.

Gains or losses on futures positions are calculated daily by the futures exchange, and trading positions are marked to market. Profits can be taken out in cash. Anyone making a loss, on the other hand, will be required to make a further payment to cover the amount of the loss. Payments to cover possible or actual losses are known as either a performance bond or margin.

There is a standard gain or loss per unit change in price (per tick movement) for any futures contract. The amount of profit or loss each day is calculated by multiplying the amount of the price movement in units or ticks by the value per tick. For example, suppose that Gamma buys 40 December eurodollar futures contracts at 94.00 and the price rises the next day to 94.20. Gamma will make a profit on the rise in price of 20 ticks. The value of one tick for this contract is $25, and so the gain on Gamma's trading position that day will be $20,000 (40 contracts × 20 ticks × $25 per tick).

Characteristics of Options on Futures

An option on a futures contract gives the right, but not the obligation, to buy (call option) or sell (put option) one futures contract at a specified price (strike price) on or before the expiry date for the option. The main difference between futures and exchange-traded options is the conditional nature of options that contrasts with contractual obligations conferred by buying or selling futures contracts.

Traded options have some of the same characteristics as futures.

- They have a standardized contract size. Each call or put option is an option to buy or sell *one* interest-rate future.
- The clearing house of the exchange acts as a counterparty to the buyer and seller in every transaction. When an option is traded between a buyer and a seller, the exchange steps in and becomes the other party to the contract for each of them. The buyer contracts to purchase the option from the futures exchange and the seller contracts to sell the option to the exchange. In this way, the buyer and the seller deal with the

exchange, and there is no counterparty risk.

- The exchange acts as a clearing house, collecting premiums from the option buyers and paying premiums to the sellers. The method of collecting premiums can differ between exchanges. On LIFFE for example, the buyer does not pay the premium on purchasing the option, and the seller does not receive the premium until later. Final settlement takes place when the option is exercised or reaches expiry, or when the option holder or option seller closes his position by selling or buying a matching option.
- The market is very liquid, so large orders can be accommodated and option-holders can sell their options easily before expiry. In the same way, futures positions are commonly unwound before settlement date.

All options on interest-rate futures are American-style and can be exercised or bought and sold at any time up to the expiry date. They can have maturities of up to two years, depending on the contract and the exchange, with expiry dates (delivery months) in March, June, September and December. For example, in January of Year 1, options on eurodollar futures may be available for delivery in March, June, September or December in Years 1 and 2. In addition, options also are traded for expiry in the next two calendar months other than March, June, September and December. For example, options on March futures are traded with expiry dates in January, February and March, when January and February are either of the next two calendar months. Similarly, options are traded for expiry in April, May and June, when April and May are either of the next two calendar months. Options on futures therefore can provide hedging cover for up to about two years, and with some options even longer, and options will be available with expiry in each of the next three months.

The expiry date for an option on a futures contract is fixed by the exchange. For options expiring in March, June, September and December, the expiry date coincides with the delivery date for the underlying futures contract.

A call option is the right to buy a futures contract at a strike price. If a call option is exercised, the holder receives a long position in the futures contract, and the exchange treats the option holder as having purchased a future at a price equal to the strike price in the option.

A put option is the right to sell a futures contract at the strike price. If a put option is exercised, the holder receives a short position in the futures contract, and the exchange treats the option holder as having sold a future at a price equal to the strike price in the option.

The method of trading options is the same as for futures. Options on futures must be purchased through a member of the exchange.

Futures trading uses a system of margins or performance bonds. These are cash payments by buyers and sellers to cover potential or actual losses on their positions. The payment of margin removes credit risk from transactions. A client of a futures exchange member will pay margin (performance bond) to the member, and the member will pay margin to the exchange (or to a clearing member of the exchange). The system of paying margin or performance bond differs slightly between exchanges, but the principle is the same for all exchanges. An initial payment is required to cover potential short-term losses on an open position in futures or options on futures. When market prices move, there will be a loss or a profit on every open position. Anyone making a loss will be required to pay further margin to cover the loss, and anyone making a gain can take the profit in cash.

Suppose that a person buys options on 10 September eurodollar interest rate futures at 94.00, and exercises the option when the market price of the September futures is 94.50. If the buyer immediately closes his/her position in September futures, and sells 10 contracts at 94.50, a profit of 50 ticks on each contract will be realized. If profits on the trading position have not already been taken out, on settlement receipts will be $12,500 ($25 per tick × 50 ticks × 10 contracts), minus the cost of the premium for the option. If someone sells an option and makes a loss, he/she will end up paying the loss through the exchange clearing system in margin payments, less the amount of the premium receivable.

Option Pricing

The *strike price* of an interest-rate option on a future is the price at which the underlying future would be acquired (call option) or sold (put option). Only a limited number of strike prices are available. They are set at standard intervals by the exchange, and the size of interval depends on the type of option.

At any time a number of different strike prices are available, at which options can be bought and sold. The intervals between strike prices usually are less than the interval between prices at which the futures contracts are traded. For example, on LIFFE the minimum price movement for the three-month sterling future is 0.005 (95.00, 95.50, 96.00 and so on), whereas exercise price intervals for options on the future are either 0.025 (95.00, 95.25, 95.50, 95.75 etc) or, for the nearest delivery months, 0.125.

The *market price* of an interest-rate option is quoted in the same way as the strike price, in index points. For short sterling options, for example, one index point or basis point is 0.01 or 0.01%. If the market price for a call option on a June three-month sterling future is 0.55, this means a premium of 55 basis points. A sterling future is for an underlying three-month deposit of £500,000 and one basis point is worth £12.50 (£500,000 × 0.01% × 3/12) and a premium of 55 basis points would cost £3,687.50 (55 × £12.50).

Prices are public knowledge because they are reported on electronic screen-based information systems.

The following examples illustrate the use of options on futures.

Options on Three-Month Sterling Futures

Options on three-month sterling deposits futures have the following features:

- The underlying financial instrument is a £500,000 three-month sterling-futures contract.

- Strike prices are quoted at intervals of 25 basis points. A number of different prices will be available at which options can be bought and sold. For example, if the current three-month sterling futures contract has a delivery month in June, and the current price for this futures contract is 93.97, options on this futures contract will have strike prices of

  9300
  9325
  9350
  9375
  9397 falls between 9375 and 9400
  9400
  9425
  9450
  9475

- Premiums, as mentioned earlier, are quoted in ticks. A tick is the minimum amount by which the price can move. In this case, one tick equals one basis point, and the value of one tick is £12.50.

Examples of quoted prices for an option in one three-month sterling-futures contract

LIFFE Short-Sterling Options

£500,000 Points of 100%

Strike price	**Calls - Settlements**		**Puts - Settlements**	
	June	**September**	**June**	**September**
9300	1.10	1.43	0.13	0.15
9325	0.90	1.23	0.18	0.20
9350	0.72	1.04	0.25	0.26
9375	0.55	0.86	0.33	0.33
9400	0.41	0.70	0.44	0.42
9425	0.29	0.56	0.57	0.53
9450	0.20	0.43	0.73	0.65
9475	0.13	0.33	0.91	0.80

Using the prices in the table, a call option for June settlement at a strike price of 9400 would cost 41 ticks. This is equivalent to
41 × £12.50 = £512.50.

If the price of the option moves to 50 ticks, the option holder could exercise the option, making a profit of nine ticks or £112.50 per option. Alternatively, it could be sold in the market to make a similar profit.

Options on US Treasury Bond Futures

The most actively traded options on futures are options on US Treasury bond futures. They have the following features:

- The underlying financial instrument is one US Treasury bond futures contract. This is $100,000 of a notional 30-year 6% coupon US government bond.
- Strike prices are quoted in intervals of two full percentage points on the Chicago Board of Trade, and one full point for the nearest delivery months.
- For example, the closing price for a US Treasury bond futures contract for June delivery might be 102-21. This price is not a decimal value but 102 27/32 because prices for these futures are shown to fractions of 1/32 of 1% on CBOT and LIFFE. Available strike prices for options on US Treasury bond futures for June delivery might be 99, 100, 101, 102, 103 and 104, and options would be traded at any of these strike prices.
- Settlement prices (premiums) for US Treasury bond futures options are quoted in sixty-fourths of 1% and one tick = 1/64 of 1%. The value of 1 tick is 1/64 of 1% of $100,000 which is $15.625.

Examples of quoted prices for an option on one US Treasury bond futures contract

US TREASURY BOND FUTURES OPTIONS
$100,000 64ths of 100%

Strike price	Calls - Settlements		Puts - Settlements	
	March	June	March	June
96	3-14	3-41	0-14	1-09
97	2-24	3-01	0-24	1-33
98	1-40	2-29	0-44	1-61
99	0-63	1-62	0-63	2-30
100	0-35	1-35	1-35	3-03
101	0-18	1-12	2-18	3-44
102	0-08	0-58	3-08	4-26
103	0-04	0-43	4-04	5-11

A call option on a futures contract with a strike price of 96 for March delivery is 3-14.

3-14 means 3% + 14/64 of 1% = (192 + 14) = 206 ticks

This would cost 206 × $15.625 = $3,218.75.

Options on long gilt futures

Options on long gilt futures have the following features:

- The underlying financial instrument is one futures contract for £100,000 of a 20-year 7% notional gilt.
- Strike prices are quoted at intervals of 0.50 (102.00, 102.50, 103.00, 103.50, and so on).
- Premiums (settlement prices) are quoted in ticks.
  One tick = 0.01 that is one hundredth of one per cent. The value of one tick = 0.01 of 1% × £100,000 = £10.

Example of quoted prices for an option on one 7% notional gilt futures contract

Options on the long gilt future might be quoted in late January for the next three exercise months as follows.

LIFFE LONG GILT FUTURES OPTIONS
£100,000 100ths of 1%

Strike		Calls			Puts	
price	Feb	Mar	Apr	Feb	Mar	Apr
10400	1.04	1.43	2.46	0.23	0.62	0.54
10450	0.71	1.13	2.11	0.40	0.83	0.69
10500	0.46	0.88	1.80	0.65	1.07	0.88
10550	0.27	0.67	1.51	0.96	1.36	1.09
10600	0.15	0.49	1.25	1.34	1.68	1.33
10650	0.07	0.36	1.02	1.76	2.05	1.60

In this example, the prices for February and March options are for options on March long gilt futures, whereas the April options are options on June futures.

Using the prices in this table, a put option on a long gilt futures option for March settlement at a strike price of 106 would cost 168. At £10 per tick, this would cost £1,680.

Using Options on Interest-Rate Futures

Banks use options on futures to hedge their own interest-rate exposures, for example their exposures on positions in the futures market.

Institutional investors use put options on government bond futures to hedge their exposure to rising interest rates and a resulting decline in the market value of the bonds in their investment portfolios.

Other companies might use options on futures as an alternative to futures, to hedge their interest-rate exposures.

- If the exposure could be hedged by selling futures, to lock in a maximum borrowing cost, the company should buy *call options* to hedge the exposure.
- If the exposure could be hedged by buying futures, to lock in a minimum rate for investments, the company should buy *put options* to hedge the exposure.

Options on futures were devised for inter-bank trading, and relatively few companies other than banks and other financial institutions use them.

Example

Suppose a company has £100 million of floating-rate debt with rollover dates every three months. Three-month LIBOR is currently 6.5% but the markets are expecting interest rates to fall in the next few months, so that the price of a June three-month sterling futures contract is 93.97 as at 15 March, reflecting an expected market rate of 100 - 93.97 = 6.03%. The table below shows options and their prices available on 15 March.

	Calls		**Puts**	
	June	**September**	**June**	**September**
9300	1.10	1.43	0.13	0.15
9325	0.90	1.23	0.18	0.20
9350	0.72	1.04	0.25	0.26
9375	0.55	0.86	0.33	0.33
9400	0.41	0.70	0.44	0.42
9425	0.29	0.56	0.57	0.53
9450	0.20	0.43	0.73	0.65
9475	0.13	0.33	0.91	0.80

Analysis

The following courses of action are open to the company.

- Sell 20 three-month sterling futures contracts at 93.97. This would lock in an effective rate of 6.03% for the three months from March on notional principal of £100 million.
- Buy 20 short sterling put options for June settlement, at a strike price of 9400. This gives the right to sell 20 three-month sterling futures contracts at 94.00. Using the prices in the table, these would cost 44 ticks each at £12.50 per tick, giving a price of £550 each and £11,000 for the total of 20.

In June, two outcomes are possible:

- If interest rates are below 6% the price of the futures contracts will rise and the company will not exercise its options. It will simply borrow at the current market rate for the next three months from the June rollover date.

- If interest rates are above 6%, the price of the futures contracts will fall and the company will exercise its options to sell futures at the strike rate. In effect the company receives a cash settlement for the profit on the sale of the options. It will pay the higher interest cost on its borrowings for the next three months from June. However, profit on the options will reduce the net interest cost for the period to 6%, ignoring the £11,000 cost of the premiums.

Buying or Selling Options on Futures

Exchange-traded interest-rate options are bought and sold in the same way as futures contracts.

Because trading on a futures exchange must be conducted through members, a company must open an account with a member who acts as a broker. Commissions payable by customers to brokers are negotiable.

Advantages of Options on Futures

Options on futures have the following advantages:

- They are exchange-traded instruments, and can be easily bought and sold.
- They provide a hedge against interest-rate exposure, but give the ability to benefit from any favorable interest-rate movement.
- Options offer high gearing in the sense that for the cost of a premium, a trader can *speculate* in large quantities of underlying capital.

Appendix: Mathematics of Option Pricing

This appendix describes the mathematics of option pricing models.

Although it is useful to study the mathematical concepts in options pricing, mathematics can be difficult to comprehend. This appendix uses simplified explanations and simplifying assumptions, where possible to make the text more comprehensible to non-mathematicians.

The purpose of this appendix is two-fold.

- To illustrate how volatility is measured, and what this measurement signifies.
- To describe a simple option pricing model for an at-the-money option that also illustrates a *delta hedging position*.

Measuring Volatility

The volatility of an interest rate can be measured mathematically from historical price data. A simplified example, based on a very short time period, will be used to illustrate the mathematics.

Example
Three-month LIBOR at a specified time on each of seven successive trading days was as follows:

Day	LIBOR
1	7.5000
2	7.5625
3	7.5625
4	7.6250
5	7.6250
6	7.6875
7	7.6250

Analysis

The first step in measuring volatility is to obtain measurements for the daily change in the interest rate. We are not trying to monitor the interest rate itself. It is the amount and direction of change that are significant.

Change in price can be measured as a price relative. This is the ratio of price on one day to the price on the previous day.

Each price relative is then converted to its natural logarithm value. You might have a calculator that computes natural logarithms. The price relatives and their natural logarithm values for the data in the example are shown in the following table.

Day	Rate (price)	Price relative	Natural logarithm of price relative
(d)		(d + 1) ÷ d	
1	7.500	-	-
2	7.5625	1.0083	0.0083
3	7.5625	1.0000	0.0000
4	7.6250	1.0083	0.0083
5	7.6250	1.0000	0.0000
6	7.6875	1.0082	0.0082
7	7.6250	0.9919	- 0.0081

The average (mean) value of the natural logarithms of the price relative is calculated as follows:

$$\frac{0.0083 + 0 + 0.0083 + 0 + 0.0082 - 0.0081}{6} = + 0.0028$$

This means the value of the natural logarithm of the price relatives is x.

We can calculate a standard deviation of the natural logarithms of the price relatives as:

$$\sigma = \sqrt{\frac{1}{(n-1)} \Sigma(x - \bar{x})^2}$$

where n is the number of natural logarithm values used to calculate the interest-rate volatility. In this example, n = 6.

x	(x - x̄)	(x - x̄)²
0.0083	0.0055	0.00003025
0.0000	- 0.0028	0.00000784
0.0083	0.0055	0.00003025
0.0000	- 0.0028	0.00000784
0.0082	0.0054	0.00002916
- 0.0081	- 0.0109	0.00011881
		0.00022415

$$\sigma = \sqrt{\frac{0.00022415}{(6-1)}}$$

= 0.00667 (approximately)

The daily volatility in the interest rate in our seven-day example is therefore 0.00667 or 0.667%.

The volatilty over a seven-day period can be used to estimate the volatility over a longer period as

$$\sigma\sqrt{d}$$

where d is the number of days in the period.

For example, if a year has 250 trading days and daily volatility in the interest rate is 0.00667, annual volatility can be estimated as 0.1055 ($0.0067 \times \sqrt{250}$), i.e. about 10.5%.

The Meaning of Volatility

Volatility is measured as a standard deviation of price relatives, and it is assumed that price changes (interest-rate changes) are normally distributed. This means that if annual volatility in an interest rate is estimated as 10.5% and today's market rate of interest is 7.625%, there is:

- a 67% probability that the interest rate in one year's time will be within the range of plus or minus 1 standard deviation of today's rate, i.e. within the range of plus or minus 10.5% from 7.625% that is in the range 6.8625% to 8.3875%
- a 95% probability that the interest rate in one year's time will be within the range of plus or minus 1.96 standard deviations of today's rate, i.e. within the range of plus or minus 20.6% from 7.625% that is in the range 6.07% to 9.20%.

In the explanation above, if you are confused by all the percentage symbols, you may prefer to think of the interest rate in basis points. For example, if volatility is 10.5% for one year and the current interest rate is 762.5 basis points, there is a 67% probability that the interest rate in one year's time will be within a range of 10.5% above or below 762.5 basis points, i.e. within the range 686.25 basis points to 838.75 basis points.

There are different ways of measuring volatility. For example, the period of time over which volatility is measured can vary. Each bank writing options could have its own measurement of volatility for any interest rate. The basic principles of volatility measurement are explained in the example above.

Changes in Volatility over Time

Volatility can be measured from historical data as a means of predicting future price changes. However over time the price volatility of an interest rate will change, sometimes by a large amount, therefore it is necessary to measure volatility continually, incorporating the most recent historical price/rate data.

Further Aspects of Volatility Measurement

Volatility measures the rate of change in a market price such as an interest rate, and also the uncertainty about the direction and size of price change.

- If an interest rate is fixed without any fluctuation at all, volatility is zero.
- If an interest rate rises by the same proportional amount every day, for example by 0.10% every day, volatility also will be zero.
- If an interest rate rises by 2% on one day and rises by 1% the next day, volatility over this two-day period will be less than if the interest rate were to rise by 2% on one day and then fall by 1% the next day. This is because volatility is higher when the *direction* as well as the amount of the price change is more variable.

Example

The three-month interbank interest rate on Day 1 for currency X is 10%. It rises by 3%, i.e. by a factor of 1.03, the next day, to 10.3%. It then rises on the following day by a further 1%, i.e. by a factor of 1.01, to 10.403%. Two-day volatility would be 1.39%, measured as follows:

Day	Rate	Price relative	Natural log		
			x	$(x - \bar{x})$	$(x - \bar{x})^2$
1	10.000	-	-	-	-
2	10.300	1.03	0.02956	0.0098	0.000096
3	10.403	1.01	0.00995	0.0098	0.000096
			0.03951		0.000192
		$\bar{x}$ =	0.01976		

$$\text{Volatility} = \sqrt{\frac{0.000192}{(2-1)}} = 0.0139 \text{ or } 1.39\%$$

If the interest rate had fallen by 1%, a factor of 1/1.01, on Day 3, from 10.03% to 10.198%, the two-day volatility would have been higher, 2.8%, measured as follows.

Day	Rate	Price relative	Natural log		
			$\bar{x}$	$(x - \bar{x})$	$(x - \bar{x})^2$
1	10.000	-	-	-	-
2	10.300	1.03	0.02956	0.0198	0.00039
3	10.198	0.99	– 0.01005	- 0.0198	0.00039
			0.01951		0.00078
		$\bar{x}$ =	0.00976		

$$\text{Volatility} = \sqrt{\frac{0.00078}{(2-1)}} = 0.028 \text{ or } 2.8\%$$

This higher price volatility reflects the difference in the price change as well as the *reverse direction* of the change, the fall in price on Day 3 after the rise in price on Day 2.

If the interest rate had *risen* by 3%, a factor of 1.03, on Day 3, from 10.3% to 10.609% that would be by the same percentage amount as on Day 2, two-day volatility would have been zero.

Day	Rate	Price relative	Natural log x	$(x - \bar{x})$	$(x - \bar{x})^2$
1	10.000	-	-	-	-
2	10.300	1.03	0.02956	0	0
3	10.609	1.03	0.02956	0	0
			0.05912		0
		$\bar{x}$ =	0.02956		

In contrast, a *fall* in the rate on Day 3, back to 10%, would give a two-day volatility of about 6%.

Using Volatility

The volatility of an interest rate affects the time value of an interest-rate option, and can be an important factor in the pricing of the option. Pricing formulae for options include volatility as a variable in the pricing equation.

A Simple Options-Pricing Model

A simple options-pricing model can be used to obtain:

- the minimum premium to be charged by the option writer, and
- the delta hedge required.

The model will be explained with a numerical example. Some simplifying assumptions have been made, but the model remains a reasonably accurate guide to pricing at-the-money options, or options that are very nearly at-the-money. The mathematics for pricing out-of-the-money options are beyond the scope of this appendix.

The example that will be used prices a call option, but the same principles can be applied to put options.

Example

A bank is asked to write a European-style lender's option for a six-month notional loan period starting in three months' time, i.e. an option on a 3 v 9 FRA. The details are as follows:

Notional principal	$100 million
Notional loan period starts	In 3 months (92 days from now)
Notional loan period ends	After 9 months (274 days from now)
Notional loan period	6 months (182 days)
Strike rate/exercise rate	At-the-money. This is about the same rate that is currently available on a 3 v 9 FRA.

We will assume that 3 v 9 FRAs are being quoted at 10.48–10.44% and that the strike rate or exercise rate for the option is 10.50%.

We will assume also that volatility in six-month dollar LIBOR is 4% flat, i.e. 4% for the three months to the start of the notional loan period. This is the equivalent to a volatility of about 17% per annum.

Analysis

Banks price options on the basis that they don't want to make an overall loss on any of the options they write. If a customer exercises an option, the bank will have to make a compensation payment. But the bank earns income in other ways.

- It receives a premium for the option.
- It can invest the premium up to the option's expiry/exercise date, and earn interest on the investment.
- It can hedge its position, to minimize its losses.

A bank writing a borrower's option can hedge its position by buying an FRA for the same notional loan period covered by the option. A bank that writes a *lender's option* can hedge its position by *selling* an FRA.

Option Writers: Hedging a Position

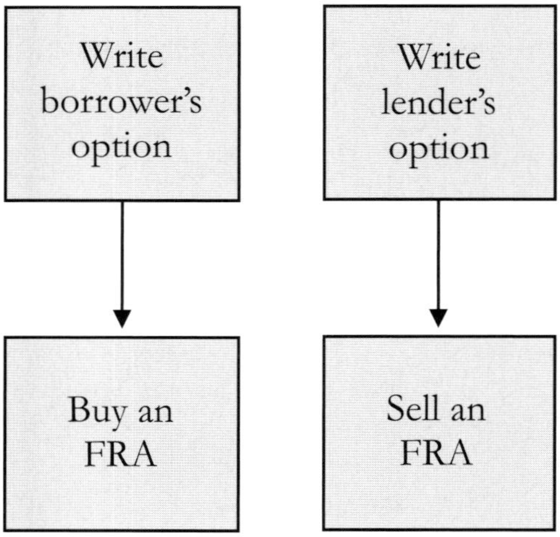

Note: An FRA is a forward contract on a notional loan, starting at a future time and for a specified period or maturity, whereby the buyer of the FRA undertakes to pay a fixed rate of interest on the loan/deposit and the seller of the FRA undertakes to receive the same fixed rate. An FRA is settled by payment of compensation, either from the FRA seller to the buyer or from the FRA buyer to the seller, on settlement date that is at the start of the notional loan period.

The bank writing the option in the above example will establish a price for the option on the basis that

- it will hedge its risk by buying an FRA, and
- if six-month LIBOR in three months' time is either 4% above or below the current rate, it will make neither a profit nor a loss on the option, taking into consideration the profit or loss on the hedging action. 4% has been chosen because it equals one times the volatility in the three-month period to the expiry of the option.

The purpose of the hedge is to create an offsetting profit if the bank makes a loss on writing the option, i.e. if the option is exercised.

The bank's possible positions, by writing an at-the-money borrower's option and buying an FRA are shown below.

Writing Interest-Rate Options: Outcomes with Hedging

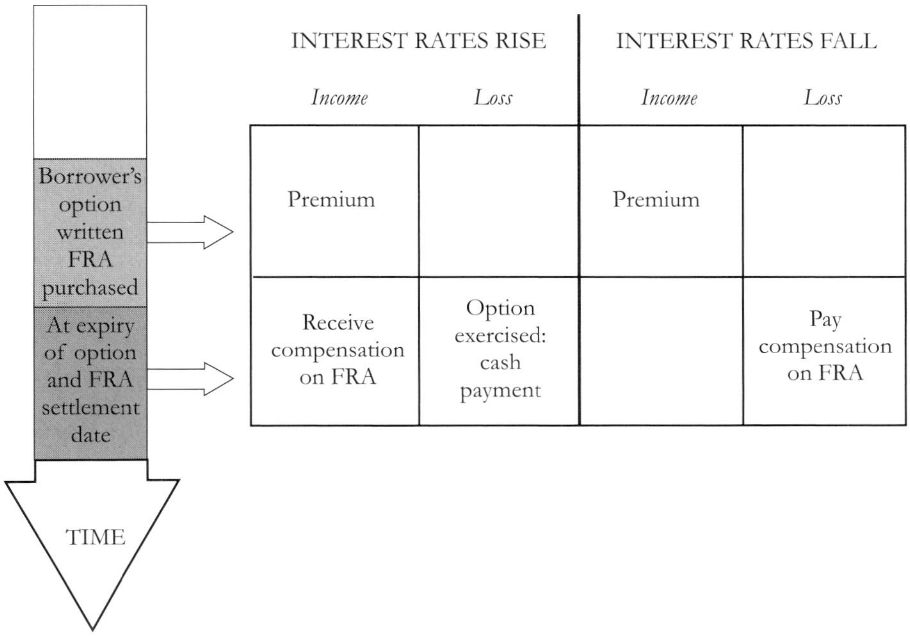

In this example, it has been assumed that the bank will provide for a maximum variation of 4%, one times the volatility, in the interest rate to the expiry of the option. The calculations that follow show how the bank will break even on its transactions even if six-month LIBOR at expiry of the option is 4% higher or 4% lower than the FRA rate when the option was written. The market's expectation should be that six-month LIBOR at expiry of the option will be more or less the same as the forward rate, i.e. the FRA rate, when the option was written.

This gives potential variation in the interest rate over the next three months as follows.

- Assumed maximum rate: 10.48% x 1.04 = 10.90%
- Assumed minimum rate: 10.48% ÷ 1.04 = 10.08%

We can price the option assuming that the six-month rate after three months will be somewhere between 10.08% and 10.90%.

Assumptions

For every $1 of notional principal in the option:

- the bank receives a premium of $P, and invests it for three months until the option expires. The investment yield on a three-month deposit is, for example, 10% per annum
- the bank can create a hedge by buying an FRA on a notional principal amount of $H. The rate on the FRA is 10.48%.

The bank writes a borrower's option on a 3 v 9 FRA at a strike rate of 10.50%. It invests this premium for three months at 10% per annum. It hedges its position by buying a 3 v 9 FRA at a fixed interest rate of 10.48%.

Possible outcomes

We can assess what will happen to the bank if the six-month interest rate is either 10.90% or 10.08% in three months' time.

Scenario A: six-month LIBOR is 10.90%

If the six-month LIBOR rate in three months' time is 10.90%, the option will be exercised.

The loss to the bank from the option being exercised will be, for each $1 of principal:

$$(10.90 - 10.50)\% \times \frac{182 \text{ days}}{360 \text{ days}}$$

$$= 0.00202222$$

The bank will have invested the premium at 10% for three months, and the investment will have built up, by the option expiry date, to:

$$P\left[1 + \left(10\% \times \frac{92}{360}\right)\right]$$

$= 1.02555P$

The bank also will make a profit on the FRA it bought, and will receive the following compensation payment from the FRA seller.

$$(10.90 - 10.48)\% \times H \times \frac{182}{360}$$

$= 0.002121233H$

For the bank to do no worse than break even, the payment it must make to the option holder in settlement of the option must be equaled by the value of the premium received, plus interest earned, and the profit on the FRA hedge.

Break even is where: 0.00202222 = 1.02555P – 0.0012233H.

Re-arranging this formula, break even is where:

0.00202222 - 1.02555P – 0.0012233H = 0

Scenario B: six-month LIBOR is 10.08%

If the six-month LIBOR rate in three months' time is 10.08%, the option will not be exercised. There will be no loss to the bank from the option. The bank also will receive the premium, and invest it for three months at 10% per annum, so that the premium with interest after three months will be 1.02555P (as above in Scenario A).

However, the bank will make a loss on its FRA position, and must pay compensation to the FRA seller. The amount of compensation payable is:

$$(10.48 - 10.08)\% \times H \times \frac{182}{360}$$

$= 0.002022H$

The breakeven position is where the premium plus interest is just sufficient to cover the bank's loss on its FRA position. This is where:

$$1.02555P = 0.002022H$$

Re-arranging this we get: Breakeven is where $1.02555P - 0.002022H = 0$

Putting the two scenarios together

We can now put the two scenarios together because we have two formulae for the bank's breakeven position. They are simultaneous equations, and we can use them to calculate a value for both P, the option premium, and H, the size of the FRA hedge.

	Six-month interest rate on Day 92			
Scenario A	10.90%	$0.0202222 - 1.02555P - 0.0021233H$	=	0
Scenario B	10.08%	$1.02555P - 0.002022H$	=	0

These simultaneous equations can be solved to get a value for H and a value for P.

- H = 0.488, i.e. the notional principal for the FRA purchased must be \$0.488 for each \$1 of notional principal in the option
- P = 0.0010, i.e. \$0.0010 per \$1 notional principal in the option

These figures mean that if the bank writes a borrower's option on a 3 v 9 FRA, as explained above, the minimum premium to ensure breakeven, given the assumptions about what interest rates might be when the option expires, must be for an option on notional principal of \$100 million:

$$P = 0.0010 \times \$100 \text{ million} = \$100{,}000$$

The bank should hedge its position using a delta hedging percentage of 0.488. The bank should buy a 3 v 9 FRA with notional principal of \$48.8 million (0.488 × \$100 million).

Note: Since the strike price of the option is at-the-money, we would expect the delta hedging percentage to be very close to 50% or 0.50.

The Black-Scholes Option-Pricing Model

In practise, banks use computer models or programmable calculators for pricing options. These computer pricing models are derived from the Black-Scholes model, or similar models. A detailed explanation of the Black-Scholes model is beyond the scope of this book.

Glossary

American Option
Option contract that can be exercised at any time up to its expiry date.

At-the-money
The strike price of an option is at-the-money when it is equal to the current market rate on the underlying loan or deposit.

Black-Scholes
A pricing model (formula) for calculating the appropriate premium for an option.

Borrower's Option
An option that gives its holder the right but not the obligation to borrow a specified quantity of notional funds for a specified term and at a specified rate of interest, from some future date on or before an expiry date.

Call Option (Interest Rates)
See also Borrower's Option. See also Cap.

Cap
An interest-rate cap is a series of borrowers' options that sets a maximum interest rate on medium-term variable-rate borrowing. An option will be exercised at each rollover date for the loan, over the term of the cap agreement if the current market rate of interest exceeds the strike price in the cap.

Caption
An option to buy a cap.

Cash Settlement
A payment by the writer of an interest-rate option to the option holder when an option is exercised. This is a payment for the difference between the strike price in the option and the market rate of interest, applied to the notional principal of the loan or deposit.

Class of Options
Exchange-traded options of the same type (call or put) and style (American or European); for example, American-style options on three-month sterling futures.

Collar
A combination of a cap and a floor. The collar holder buys a cap and sells a floor, or buys a floor and sells a cap, to fix a maximum and minimum interest rate on borrowing or lending. The advantage of a collar over a cap or floor is a lower premium.

Compensating Payment
See Cash Settlement.

Contract for Difference
A contract that is cash-settled rather than settled by physical delivery. Examples of contracts for difference are OTC interest-rate options, short-term interest-rate futures and FRAs.

Delta
A ratio measuring the percentage change in the value of an option (option premium) for a given change in the interest rate. An option's delta will have a value in the range from zero (deeply out-of the-money) to 1 (deeply in-the-money).

Delta Hedge
A system of hedging exposures to options positions whereby the hedge involves buying or selling a quantity of the underlying instrument to which the option relates. In the case of interest-rate options, a delta hedge involves buying or selling FRAs or swaps. The size of the hedge is determined by the option's delta.

Derivative

A financial security, such as an option, swap or future, whose value is derived in part from the value and characteristics of another underlying security. In the case of interest-rate options, the underlying security is a notional loan or deposit.

European Option

Option contract that can be exercised only on its expiry date. Options on interest-rate futures are all American style.

Exercise an Interest-Rate Option

To enforce the right to borrow (call option) or lend (put option) the notional principal in the option agreement, obliging the option writer to lend (call option) or borrow (put option) the funds at the strike price. In practise, there is a cash settlement between the parties, not an actual loan or deposit transaction.

Exercise Price

Also called the strike price or strike rate. For interest-rate options, this is the interest rate at which the principal can be borrowed (call option) or lent (put option).

Expiry Date (Expiration Date)

The last date on which an option can be exercised before it expires.

Expiry Month (Expiration Month)

The month in which an option expires. Used to identify a series of traded options.

Floor

A series of lenders' options that sets a minimum interest-rate income for medium-term variable-rate lending or investments. An option will be exercised at each interest-rate reset date during the term of the floor agreement if the current market rate of interest is below the strike price of the floor.

FRA

Forward rate areement. An over-the-counter agreement by which an interest rate is fixed now for buying/selling a future notional interest-earning deposit, starting at a specified time in the futire and having a specified notional principal amount and maturity. It is a forward contract on a short-term interest rate.

Future

An interest-rate future is an exchange-traded contract for the purchase and sale of a standard quantity of a money-market instrument, e.g. a three-month deposit, or government bonds, at an agreed interest rate or price, and for delivery at a specified future date.

Gamma

For interest-rate options, gamma is the ratio of the rate of change in an option's delta to the rate of change in the underlying interest rate.

Hedge

Action to reduce or limit a financial risk such as an exposure to an adverse movement in interest rates. Interest-rate options can provide a hedge against movements in short-term (money-market) interest rates.

Interest Rate Guarantee (IRG)

Another name for an interest-rate option.

In-the-money

An interest-rate option's strike price is in-the-money when it is more favorable to the option holder than the current market interest rate; for example, a borrower's option is in-the-money if the strike price is below the current market rate of interest.

Intrinsic Value

Together with time value, intrinsic value makes up the premium (purchase price) of an option. Intrinsic value is the amount by which the option is in-the-money and is the value of the difference between the strike price and the current market rate of interest.

Lender's Option

A put option that gives its holder the right but not the obligation to deposit a specified quantity of notional principal for a specified term and at a specified rate of interest, from a period starting on or before a specified future date.

LIBOR

London Interbank Offered Rate, a benchmark money-market rate for setting interest rates on variable-rate loans in sterling and the dollar. It is used to set a rate for short-term interbank lending between top-rated banks.

Liquidity

A market is liquid when it has a high level of trading activity, allowing buying and selling with minimum price changes for individual transactions.

Out-of-the-money

An interest-rate option's strike price is out-of-the-money when it is less favorable to the option holder than the current market rate of interest. For example, a lender's option is out-of-the-money when its strike price is below the current market rate of interest. If an option is out-of-the-money on its expiry date, it will not be exercised.

Premium

The price of an option contract, payable for the purchase of the option.

Put option (Interest-Rate Option)

See Lender's Option. See also Floor.

Series

A series of exchange-traded options consists of all options of the same class with the same strike price and the same expiry date.

Speculator

An investor who seeks to make profits by buying and selling financial instruments in anticipation of future changes in market prices.

Strike Price or Strike Rate

See Exercise price.

Style of Option
Distinction between American and European options.

Theta
A ratio measuring the percentage change in an option's price for a given percentage change in the time to expiry of the option.

Time Decay
Fall in the time value of an option as it approaches its expiry date.

Time Value
With intrinsic value, time value makes up the premium (purchase price) of an option. Time value is that part of the premium attributed to factors such as the time to expiry date and uncertainty about interest-rate movements (volatility) over that time. Time value can be measured as the difference between the premium and the intrinsic value.

Volatility
Measurement/description of price volatility in the underlying security. For interest-rate options, volatility refers to the historical or potential future movements in the interest rate.

Writer
Seller of an option contract.

Zero-Cost Collar
An interest-rate collar agreement where no premium is payable. *See also Collar.*

Index

Notes

Notes

Notes